The History of Thomas Ellwood Written

Thomas Ellwood

The History of Thomas Ellwood Written by

Table of Contents

The History of Thomas Ellwood Written by

Thomas Ellwood

Kessinger Publishing reprints thousands of hard−to−find books!

Visit us at http://www.kessinger.net

THE HISTORY OF THOMAS ELLWOOD WRITTEN BY HIMSELF

INTRODUCTION BY HENRY MORLEY

The life of the simple Quaker, Thomas Ellwood, to whom the pomps and shows of earth were nowhere so vain as in association with the spiritual life of man, may serve as companion to another volume in this Library, the "Life of Wolsey" by George Cavendish, who, as a gentleman of the great prelate's household, made part of his pomp, but had heart to love him in his pride and in his fall. "The History of Thomas Ellwood, written by Himself," is interesting for the frankness with which it makes Thomas Ellwood himself known to us; and again, for the same frank simplicity that brings us nearer than books usually bring us to a living knowledge of some features of a bygone time; and yet again, because it helps us a little to come near to Milton in his daily life. He would be a good novelist who could invent as pleasant a book as this unaffected record of a quiet life touched by great influences in eventful times.

Thomas Ellwood, who was born in 1639, in the reign of Charles the First, carried the story of his life in this book to the year 1683, when he was forty–four years old. He outlived the days of trouble here recorded, enjoyed many years of peace, and died, near the end of Queen Anne's reign, aged 74, on the first of March 1713, in his house at Hunger Hill, by Amersham. He was eleven years younger than John Bunyan, and years younger than George Fox, the founder of that faithful band of worshippers known as the Society of Friends. They turned from all forms and ceremonies that involved untruth or insincerity, now the temple of God in man's body, and, as Saint Paul said the Corinthians, "Know ye not that ye are the temple of God, and that the Spirit of God dwelleth in you," they sought to bring Christ into their hearts, and speak and act as if Christ was within governing their words and actions. They would have no formal prayers, no formal preaching, but sought to speak with each other as the Spirit prompted, soul to soul. They would not, when our plural pronoun "you" was still only plural, speak to one man as if he were two or more. They swore not at all; but their "Yea" and "Nay" were known to be more binding than the oaths of many of their persecutors. And as they would not go through the required form of swearing allegiance to the Government whenever called upon to do so, they were continually liable to penalties of imprisonment when imprisonment too often meant jail fever, misery, and death. George Fox began his teaching when Ellwood was eight years old. Ellwood was ten years old when Fox was first imprisoned at Nottingham, and the offences of his followers against established forms led, as he says, to "great rage, blows, punchings, beatings, and imprisonments." Of what this rage meant, and of the spirit in which it was endured, we learn much from the History of Thomas Ellwood.

Isaac Penington, whose influence upon young Ellwood's mind is often referred to in this book, was born in the year of Shakespeare's death, and had joined the Society of Friends in 1658, when his own age was forty–two and Ellwood's was nineteen. He was the son of Alderman Isaac Penington, a Puritan member for the City of London, who announced, at a time in the year 1640 when the Parliament was in sore need of money, that his constituents had subscribed £21,000 to a loan, which the members of the House then raised to £90,000, by rising, one after another, to give their personal bonds each for a thousand pounds. Isaac Penington the son, whom Ellwood loved as a friend and reverenced as a father, became a foremost worker and writer in the Society of Friends. In a note upon him, written after his death, Thomas Ellwood said that "in his family he was a true pattern of goodness and piety; to his wife he was a most affectionate husband; to his children, a loving and tender father; to his servants, a mild and gentle master; to his friends, a firm and fast friend; to the poor, compassionate and open–hearted; and to all, courteous and kind?' In 1661 he was committed to Aylesbury gaol for worshipping God in his own house (holding a conventicle), "where," says Ellwood in that little testimony which he wrote after his friend's death, "for seventeen weeks, great part of it in winter, he was kept in a cold and very incommodious room, without a chimney; from which hard usage his tender body contracted so great and violent a distemper that, for several weeks after, he was not able to turn himself in bed." "His second imprisonment," says Ellwood, "was in the year 1664, being taken out of a meeting, when he with others were peaceably waiting on the Lord, and sent to Aylesbury gaol, where he again remained a prisoner between seventeen and eighteen weeks.

"His third imprisonment was in the year 1665, being taken up, with many others, in the open street of Amersham, as they were carrying and accompanying the body of a deceased Friend to the grave. From hence he was sent again to Aylesbury gaol; but this commitment being in order to banishment, was but for a month, or thereabouts.

"His fourth imprisonment was in the same year 1665, about a month after his releasement from the former. Hitherto his commitment had been by the civil magistrates; but now, that he might experience the severity of each, he fell into the military hands. A rude soldier, without any other warrant than what he carried in his scabbard, came to his house, and told him he came to fetch him before Sir Philip Palmer, one of the deputy–lieutenants of the county. He meekly went, and was by him sent with a guard of soldiers to Aylesbury gaol, with a kind of mittimus, importing 'That the gaoler should receive and keep him in safe custody during the pleasure of the Earl of Bridgewater,' who had, it seems, conceived so great, as well as unjust, displeasure against this innocent man, that, although (it being the sickness year) the plague was suspected to be in the gaol, he would not be prevailed with only to permit Isaac Penington to be removed to another house in the town, and there kept prisoner until the gaol was clear. Afterwards, a prisoner dying in the gaol of the plague, the gaoler's wife, her husband being absent, gave leave to Isaac Penington to remove to another house, where he was shut up for six weeks; after which, by the procurement of the Earl of Ancram, a release was sent from the said Philip Palmer, by which he was discharged, after he had suffered imprisonment three–quarters of a year, with apparent hazard of his life, and that for no offence."

This was not the end of the troubles of Ellwood's patron and friend. He had been home only three weeks when "the said Philip Palmer" seized him again, dragged him out of bed, sent him, without any cause shown, to Aylesbury gaol, and kept him a year and a half prisoner "in rooms so cold, damp, and unhealthy, that it went very near to cost him his life, and procured him so great a distemper that he lay weak of it several months. At length a relation of his wife, by an *habeas corpus*, removed him to the King's Bench bar, where (with the wonder of the court that a man should he so long imprisoned for nothing) he was at last released in the year 1668." "Paradise Lost" had appeared in the year before. Yet a sixth imprisonment followed in 1670, when Penington, visiting some Friends in Reading gaol, was seized and carried before Sir William Armorer, a justice of the peace, who sent him back to share their sufferings. Penington died in 1679.

Of Thomas Ellwood's experience as reader to Milton, and of Milton's regard for the gentle Quaker, the book tells its own tale. I will only add one comment upon an often-quoted incident that it contains. When Milton gave his young friend—then twenty-six years old—the manuscript of "Paradise Lost" to read, his desire could only have been to learn what comprehension of his purpose there would be in a young man sincerely religious, as intelligent as most, and with a taste for verse, though not much of a poet. The observation Ellwood made, of which he is proud because of its consequence, might well cause Milton to be silent for a little while, and then change the conversation. It showed that the whole aim of the poem had been missed. Its crown is in the story of redemption, Paradise Found, the better Eden, the "Paradise within thee, happier far." Milton had applied his test, and learnt— what every great poet has to learn—that he must trust more to the vague impression of truth, beauty, and high thought, that can be made upon thousands of right-hearted men and women, than to the clear, full understanding of his work. The noblest aims of the true artist can make themselves felt by all, though understood by few. Few know the secrets of the sunshine, although all draw new life from the sun. When Milton—who, with his habitual gentleness, never allowed Ellwood to suspect that he had missed the whole purpose of "Paradise Lost"— showed him "Paradise Regained," and made him happy by telling him that he caused it to be written; he showed him a poem that expanded the closing thought of "Paradise Lost" into an image of the Paradise within, that is to be obtained only by an imitation of Christ under all forms of our temptation.

Of Ellwood's life after the year in which he ends his own account of it, let it suffice to say, that he wrote earnest, gentle books in support of his opinions and against the persecution of them. He lived retired until the year 1688, and occupied himself with an attempt at a *Davideis*, a Life of David in verse. He had not then seen Cowley's. Ellwood carried on his verses to the end of David's life, and published them in 1712. When George Fox died, in 1690, Thomas Ellwood transcribed his journal for the press, and printed it next year in folio, prefixing an account of Fox. He was engaged afterwards in controversy with George Keith, a seceder from the Friends. His intellectual activity continued unabated to the end. In 1709 he suffered distraint for tithes; goods to the value of £24 10s. being taken for a due of about £14, after which the distrainers "brought him still in debt, and wanted more."

Ellwood's life was healthy, except that he was asthmatic towards the end. His wife died five years before him. Of her, J. Wyeth, citizen of London, who was the editor of

"Ellwood's History of his Life," and wrote its sequel, says that she was "a solid, weighty woman." But the context shows that he means those adjectives to be read in a spiritual sense. "The liberal soul shall be made fat," says Solomon.

H. M.
November 1885.

THE HISTORY OF THOMAS ELLWOOD—WRITTEN BY HIMSELF

Although my station, not being so eminent either in the church of Christ or in the world as others who have moved in higher orbs, may not afford such considerable remarks as theirs, yet inasmuch as in the course of my travels through this vale of tears I have passed through various and some uncommon exercises, which the Lord hath been graciously pleased to support me under and conduct me through, I hold it a matter excusable at least, if not commendable, to give the world some little account of my life, that in recounting the many deliverances and preservations which the Lord hath vouchsafed to work for me, both I, by a grateful acknowledgment thereof and return of thanksgivings unto him therefor, may in some measure set forth His abundant goodness to me, and others, whose lot it may be to tread the same path and fall into the same or like exercises, may be encouraged to persevere in the way of holiness, and with full assurance of mind to trust in the Lord, whatsoever trials may befall them.

To begin therefore with mine own beginning, I was born in the year of our Lord 1639, about the beginning of the eighth month, so far as I have been able to inform myself, for the parish register, which relates to the time not of birth but of baptism, as they call it, is not to be relied on.

The History of Thomas Ellwood Written by

The place of my birth was a little country town called Crowell, situate in the upper side of Oxfordshire, three miles eastward from Thame, the nearest market town.

My father's name was Walter Ellwood, and my mother's maiden name was Elizabeth Potman, both well descended, but of declining families. So that what my father possessed (which was a pretty estate in lands, and more as I have heard in moneys) he received, as he had done his name Walter, from his grandfather Walter Gray, whose daughter and only child was his mother.

In my very infancy, when I was but about two years old, I was carried to London; for the civil war between King and Parliament breaking then forth, my father, who favoured the Parliament side, though he took not arms, not holding himself safe at his country habitation, which lay too near some garrisons of the King's, betook himself to London, that city then holding for the Parliament.

There was I bred up, though not without much difficulty, the city air not agreeing with my tender constitution, and there continued until Oxford was surrendered, and the war in appearance ended.

In this time my parents contracted an acquaintance and intimate friendship with the Lady Springett, who being then the widow of Sir William Springett, who died in the Parliament service, was afterwards the wife of Isaac Penington, eldest son of Alderman Penington, of London. And this friendship devolving from the parents to the children, I became an early and particular playfellow to her daughter Gulielma; being admitted, as such, to ride with her in her little coach, drawn by her footman about Lincoln's Inn Fields.

I mention this in this place because the continuation of that acquaintance and friendship, having been an occasional means of my being afterwards brought to the knowledge of the blessed TRUTH, I shall have frequent cause, in the course of the following discourse, to make honourable mention of that family, to which I am under so many and great obligations.

Soon after the surrender of Oxford my father returned to his estate at Crowell, which by that time he might have need enough to look after, having spent, I suppose, the greatest part of the moneys which had been left him by his grandfather in maintaining himself and his family at a high rate in London.

My elder brother (for I had one brother and two sisters, all elder than myself) was, while we lived in London, boarded at a private school, in the house of one Francis Atkinson, at a place called Hadley, near Barnet, in Hertfordshire, where he had made some good proficiency in the Latin and French tongues. But after we had left the city, and were re-settled in the country, he was taken from that private school and sent to the free school at Thame, in Oxfordshire.

Thither also was I sent as soon as my tender age would permit; for I was indeed but young when I went, and yet seemed younger than I was, by reason of my low and little stature. For it was held for some years a doubtful point whether I should not have proved a dwarf. But after I was arrived at the fifteenth year of my age, or thereabouts, I began to shoot up, and gave not up growing till I had attained the middle size and stature of men.

At this school, which at that time was in good reputation, I profited apace, having then a natural propensity to learning; so that at the first reading over of my lesson I commonly made myself master of it; and yet, which is strange to think of, few boys in the school wore out more birch than I. For though I was never, that I remember, whipped upon the score of not having my lesson ready, or of not saying it well, yet being a little busy boy, full of spirit, of a working head and active hand, I could not easily conform myself to the grave and sober rules and, as I then thought, severe orders of the school, but was often playing one waggish prank or other among my fellow-scholars, which subjected me to correction, so that I have come under the discipline of the rod twice in a forenoon; which yet brake no bones.

Had I been continued at this school, and in due time preferred to a higher, I might in likelihood have been a scholar, for I was observed to have a genius apt to learn. But my father having, so soon as the republican government began to settle, accepted the office of a justice of the peace (which was no way beneficial, but merely honorary, and every way expensive), and put himself into a port and course of living agreeably thereunto, and having also removed my brother from Thame school to Merton College in Oxford, and entered him there in the highest and most chargeable condition of a Fellow Commoner, he found it needful to retrench his expenses elsewhere, the hurt of which fell upon me. For he thereupon took me from school, to save the charge of maintaining me there; which was somewhat like plucking green fruit from the tree, and laying it by before it was come to its due ripeness, which will thenceforth shrink and wither, and lose that little juice and relish which it began to have.

Even so it fared with me. For being taken home when I was but young, and before I was well settled in my studies (though I had made a good progress in the Latin tongue, and was entered in the Greek) being left too much to myself, to ply or play with my books, or without them, as I pleased, I soon shook hands with my books by shaking my books out of my hands, and laying them by degrees quite aside, and addicted myself to such youthful sports and pleasures as the place afforded and my condition could reach unto.

By this means, in a little time I began to lose that little learning I had acquired at school, and by a continued disuse of my books became at length so utterly a stranger to learning, that I could not have read, far less have understood, a sentence in Latin: which I was so sensible of that I warily avoided reading to others, even in an English book, lest, if I should meet with a Latin word, I should shame myself by mispronouncing it.

Thus I went on, taking my swing in such vain courses as were accounted harmless recreations, entertaining my companions and familiar acquaintance with pleasant discourses in our conversations, by the mere force of mother–wit and natural parts, without the help of school cultivation; and was accounted good company too.

But I always sorted myself with persons of ingenuity, temperance, and sobriety; for I loathed scurrilities in conversation, and had a natural aversion to immoderate drinking. So that in the time of my greatest vanity I was preserved from profaneness and the grosser evils of the world, which rendered me acceptable to persons of the best note in that country then. I often waited on the Lord Wenman at his house, Thame Park, about two miles from Crowell, where I lived; to whose favour I held myself entitled in a twofold respect, both as my mother was nearly related to his lady, and as he had been pleased to bestow his name upon me, when he made large promises for me at the font. He was a person of great honour and virtue, and always gave me a kind reception at his table, how often soever I came. And I have cause to think I should have received from this lord some advantageous preferment in this world, as soon as he had found me capable of it (though betwixt him and my father there was not then so good an understanding as might have been wished), had I not been, in a little time after, called into the service of the best and highest Lord, and thereby lost the favour of all my friends, relations, and acquaintance of this world. To the account of which most happy exchange I hasten, and therefore willingly pass over many particularities of my youthful life. Yet one passage I am willing to mention, for the effect it had upon me afterwards, which was thus.

My father being then in the Commission of the Peace, and going to a Petty Sessions at Watlington, I waited on him thither. And when we came near the town, the coachman, seeing a nearer and easier way (than the common road) through a corn–field, and that it was wide enough for the wheels to run without damaging the corn, turned down there; which being observed by a husbandman who was at plough not far off, he ran to us, and stopping the coach, poured forth a mouthful of complaints, in none of the best language, for driving over the corn. My father mildly answered him, "That if there was an offence committed, he must rather impute it to his servant than himself, since he neither directed him to drive that way, nor knew which way he drove." Yet added, "That he was going to such an inn at the town, whither if he came he would make him full satisfaction for whatsoever damage he had sustained thereby." And so on we went, the man venting his discontent, as he went back, in angry accents. At the town, upon inquiry, we understood that it was a way often used, and without damage, being broad enough; but that it was not the common road, which yet lay not far from it, and was also good enough; wherefore my father bid his man drive home that way.

It was late in the evening when we returned, and very dark; and this quarrelsome man, who had troubled himself and us in the morning, having gotten another lusty fellow like himself to assist him, waylaid us in the night, expecting we would return the same way we came. But when they found we did not, but took the common way, they, angry that they were disappointed, and loth to lose their purpose (which was to put an abuse upon us), coasted over to us in the dark, and laying hold on the horses' bridles, stopped them from going on. My father, asking his man what the reason was that he went not on, was answered, "That there were two men at the horses' heads, who held them back, and would not suffer them to go forward." Whereupon my father, opening the boot, stepped out, and I followed close at his heels. Going up to the place where the men stood, he demanded of them the meaning of this assault. They said, "We were upon the corn." We knew by the route we were not on the corn, but in the common way, and told them so; but they told us, "They were resolved they would not let us go on any farther, but would make us go back again." My father endeavoured by gentle reasoning to persuade them to forbear, and not run themselves farther into the danger of the law, which they were run too far into already; but they rather derided him for it. Seeing therefore fair means would not work upon them, he spake more roughly to them, charging them to deliver their clubs (for each of them had a great club in his hand, somewhat like those which are called quarter–staves): they thereupon, laughing, told him, "They did not bring them thither for that end." Thereupon my father, turning his head to me, said, "Tom, disarm them."

10

I stood ready at his elbow, waiting only for the word of command. For being naturally of a bold spirit, full then of youthful heat, and that, too, heightened by the sense I had, not only of the abuse, but insolent behaviour of those rude fellows, my blood began to boil, and my fingers itched, as the saying is, to be dealing with them. Wherefore, stepping boldly forward to lay hold on the staff of him that was nearest to me, I said, "Sirrah, deliver your weapon." He thereupon raised his club, which was big enough to have knocked down an ox, intending no doubt to have knocked me down with it, as probably he would have done, had I not, in the twinkling of an eye, whipped out my rapier, and made a pass upon him. I could not have failed running of him through up to the hilt had he stood his ground, but the sudden and unexpected sight of my bright blade glittering in the dark night, did so amaze and terrify the man, that, slipping aside, he avoided my thrust, and letting his staff sink, betook himself to his heels for safety; which his companion seeing, fled also. I followed the former as fast as I could, but *timor addidit alas* (fear gave him wings), and made him swiftly fly; so that, although I was accounted very nimble, yet the farther we ran the more ground he gained on me; so that I could not overtake him, which made me think he took shelter under some bush, which he knew where to find, though I did not. Meanwhile, the coachman, who had sufficiently the outside of a man, excused himself from intermeddling under pretence that he durst not leave his horses, and so left me to shift for myself; and I was gone so far beyond my knowledge, that I understood not which way I was to go, till by halloing, and being halloed to again, I was directed where to find my company.

We had easy means to have found out who these men were (the principal of them having been in the daytime at the inn, and both quarrelled with the coachman, and threatened to be even with him when he went back); but since they came off no better in their attempt, my father thought it better not to know them, than to oblige himself to a prosecution of them.

At that time, and for a good while after, I had no regret upon my mind for what I had done, and designed to have done, in this case, but went on in a sort of bravery, resolving to kill, if I could, any man that should make the like attempt or put any affront on us; and for that reason seldom went afterwards upon those public services without a loaded pistol in my pocket. But when it pleased the Lord, in his infinite goodness, to call me out of the spirit and ways of the world, and give me the knowledge of his saving truth, whereby the actions of my fore−past life were set in order before me, a sort of horror seized on me, when I considered how near I had been to the staining of my hands with human blood.

And whensoever afterwards I went that way, and indeed as often since as the matter has come into my remembrance, my soul has blessed the Lord for my deliverance, and thanksgivings and praises have arisen in my heart (as now at the relating of it, they do) to Him who preserved and withheld me from shedding man's blood. Which is the reason for which I have given this account of that action, that others may be warned by it.

About this time my dear and honoured mother, who was indeed a woman of singular worth and virtue, departed this life, having a little before heard of the death of her eldest son, who (falling under the displeasure of my father for refusing to resign his interest in an estate which my father sold, and thereupon desiring that he might have leave to travel, in hopes that time and absence might work a reconciliation) went into Ireland with a person powerful there in those times, by whose means he was quickly preferred to a place of trust and profit, but lived not long to enjoy it.

I mentioned before, that during my father's abode in London, in the time of the civil wars, he contracted a friendship with the Lady Springett, then a widow, and afterwards married to Isaac Penington, Esq., to continue which he sometimes visited them at their country lodgings, as at Datchet, and at Causham Lodge, near Reading. And having heard that they were come to live upon their own estate at Chalfont, in Buckinghamshire, about fifteen miles from Crowell, he went one day to visit them there, and to return at night, taking me with him.

But very much surprised we were when, being come thither, we first heard, then found, they were become Quakers; a people we had no knowledge of, and a name we had till then scarce heard of.

So great a change, from a free, debonair, and courtly sort of behaviour, which we formerly had found them in, to so strict a gravity as they now received us with did not a little amuse us, and disappoint our expectation of such a pleasant visit as we used to have, and had now promised ourselves. Nor could my father have any opportunity, by a private conference with them, to understand the ground or occasion of this change, there being some other strangers with them (related to Isaac Penington), who came that morning from London to visit them also.

For my part I sought and at length found means to cast myself into the company of the daughter, whom I found gathering some flowers in the garden, attended by her maid, who was also a Quaker. But when I addressed myself to her after my accustomed manner, with intention to engage her in some discourse which might introduce conversation on the footing of our former acquaintance, though she treated me with a courteous mien, yet, as young as she was, the gravity of her look and behaviour struck such an awe upon me, that I found myself not so much master of myself as to pursue any further converse with her. Wherefore, asking pardon for my boldness in having intruded myself into her private walks, I withdrew, not without some disorder (as I thought at least) of mind.

We stayed dinner, which was very handsome, and lacked nothing to recommend it to me but the want of mirth and pleasant discourse, which we could neither have with them, nor by reason of them, with one another amongst ourselves; the weightiness that was upon their spirits and countenances keeping down the lightness that would have been up in us. We stayed, notwithstanding, till the rest of the company took leave of them, and then we also, doing the same, returned, not greatly satisfied with our journey, nor knowing what in particular to find fault with.

Yet this good effect that visit had upon my father, who was then in the Commission of the Peace, that it disposed him to a more favourable opinion of and carriage towards those people when they came in his way, as not long after one of them did. For a young man, who lived in Buckinghamshire, came on a first–day to the church (so called) at a town called Chinner, a mile from Crowell, having, it seems, a pressure on his mind to say something to the minister of that parish. He being an acquaintance of mine, drew me sometimes to hear him, as it did then. The young man stood in the aisle before the pulpit all the time of the sermon, not speaking a word till the sermon and prayer after it were ended, and then spoke a few words to the priest, of which all that I could hear was, "That the prayer of the wicked is abomination to the Lord, and that God heareth not sinners."

Somewhat more, I think, he did say, which I could not distinctly hear for the noise the people made; and more probably he would have said, had he not been interrupted by the officers, who took him into custody, and led him out in order to carry him before my father.

When I understood that, I hastened home, that I might give my father a fair account of the matter before they came. I told him the young man behaved himself quietly and peaceably, spoke not a word till the minister had quite done his service, and that what he then spoke was but short, and was delivered without passion or ill language. This I knew

13

would furnish my father with a fair ground whereon to discharge the man if he would.

And accordingly when they came, and made a high complaint against the man (who said little for himself), my father, having examined the officers who brought him—what the words that he spoke were (which they did not well agree in), and at what time he spoke them (which they all agreed to be after the minister had done), and then, whether he gave the minister any reviling language, or endeavoured to raise a tumult among the people (which they could not charge him with); not finding that he had broken the law, he counselled the young man to be careful that he did not make or occasion any public disturbance, and so dismissed him; which I was glad of.

Some time after this, my father, having gotten some further account of the people called Quakers, and being desirous to be informed concerning their principles, made another visit to Isaac Penington and his wife, at their house called the Grange, in Peter's Chalfont, and took both my sisters and me with him.

It was in the tenth month, in the year 1659, that we went thither, where we found a very kind reception, and tarried some days; one day at least the longer, for that while we were there a meeting was appointed at a place about a mile from thence, to which we were invited to go, and willingly went.

It was held in a farmhouse called the Grove, which having formerly been a gentleman's seat, had a very large hall, and that well filled.

To this meeting came Edward Burrough, besides other preachers, as Thomas Curtis and James Naylor, but none spoke there at that time but Edward Burrough, next to whom, as it were under him, it was my lot to sit on a stool by the side of a long table on which he sat, and I drank in his words with desire; for they not only answered my understanding, but warmed my heart with a certain heat, which I had not till then felt from the ministry of any man.

When the meeting was ended our friends took us home with them again; and after supper, the evenings being long, the servants of the family (who were Quakers) were called in, and we all sat down in silence. But long we had not so sat before Edward Burrough began to speak among us. And although he spoke not long, yet what he said did touch, as I suppose, my father's (religious) copyhold, as the phrase is. And he having been from his youth a professor, though not joined in that which is called close communion with any one sort, and valuing himself upon the knowledge he esteemed himself to have in the various notions of each profession, thought he had now a fair opportunity to display his knowledge, and thereupon began to make objections against what had been delivered.

The subject of the discourse was, "The universal free grace of God to all mankind," to which he opposed the Calvinistic tenet of particular and personal predestination; in defence of which indefensible notion he found himself more at a loss than he expected. Edward Burrough said not much to him upon it, though what he said was close and cogent; but James Naylor interposing, handled the subject with so much perspicuity and clear demonstration, that his reasoning seemed to be irresistible; and so I suppose my father found it, which made him willing to drop the discourse.

As for Edward Burrough, he was a brisk young man, of a ready tongue, and might have been, for aught I then knew, a scholar, which made me the less to admire his way of reasoning. But what dropt from James Naylor had the greater force upon me, because he looked but like a plain simple countryman, having the appearance of a husbandman or a shepherd.

As my father was not able to maintain the argument on his side, so neither did they seem willing to drive it to an extremity on their side; but treating him in a soft and gentle manner, did after a while let fall the discourse, and then we withdrew to our respective chambers.

The next morning we prepared to return home (that is, my father, my younger sister, and myself, for my elder sister was gone before by the stage–coach to London), and when, having taken our leaves of our friends, we went forth, they, with Edward Burrough, accompanying us to the gate, he there directed his speech in a few words to each of us severally, according to the sense he had of our several conditions. And when we were gone off, and they gone in again, they asking him what he thought of us, he answered them, as they afterwards told me, to this effect: "As for the old man, he is settled on his lees, and the young woman is light and airy; but the young man is reached, and may do well if he does not lose it." And surely that which he said to me, or rather that spirit in which he spoke it, took such fast hold on me, that I felt sadness and trouble come over me, though I did not distinctly understand what I was troubled for. I knew not what I ailed, but I knew I ailed something more than ordinary, and my heart was very heavy.

I found it was not so with my father and sister, for as I rode after the coach I could hear them talk pleasantly one to the other; but they could not discern how it was with me, because I, riding on horseback, kept much out of sight.

By the time we got home it was night; and the next day, being the first day of the week, I went in the afternoon to hear the minister of Chinner, and this was the last time I ever went to hear any of that function. After the sermon I went with him to his house, and in a freedom of discourse, which, from a certain intimacy that was between us, I commonly used with him, told him where I had been, what company I had met with there, and what observations I had made to myself thereupon. He seemed to understand as little of them as I had done before, and civilly abstained from casting any unhandsome reflections on them.

I had a desire to go to another meeting of the Quakers, and bade my father's man inquire if there was any in the country thereabouts. He thereupon told me he had heard at Isaac Penington's that there was to be a meeting at High Wycombe on Thursday next.

Thither therefore I went, though it was seven miles from me; and that I might be rather thought to go out a–coursing than to a meeting, I let my greyhound run by my horse's side.

When I came there, and had set up my horse at an inn, I was at a loss how to find the house where the meeting was to be. I knew it not, and was ashamed to ask after it; wherefore, having ordered the ostler to take care of my dog, I went into the street and stood at the inn gate, musing with myself what course to take. But I had not stood long ere I saw a horseman riding along the street, whom I remembered I had seen before at Isaac Penington's, and he put up his horse at the same inn. Him therefore I resolved to follow, supposing he was going to the meeting, as indeed he was.

Being come to the house, which proved to be John Raunce's, I saw the people sitting together in an outer room; wherefore I stepped in and sat down on the first void seat, the end of a bench just within the door, having my sword by my side and black clothes on, which drew some eyes upon me. It was not long ere one stood up and spoke, whom I was afterwards well acquainted with; his name was Samuel Thornton, and what he said was very suitable and of good service to me, for it reached home as if it had been directed to me.

16

As soon as ever the meeting was ended and the people began to rise, I, being next the door, stepped out quickly, and hastening to my inn, took horse immediately homewards, and (so far as I remember) my having been gone was not taken notice of by my father.

This latter meeting was like the clinching of a nail, confirming and fastening in my mind those good principles which had sunk into me at the former. My understanding began to open, and I felt some stirrings in my breast, tending to the work of a new creation in me. The general trouble and confusion of mind, which had for some days lain heavy upon me and pressed me down, without a distinct discovery of the particular cause for which it came, began now to wear off, and some glimmerings of light began to break forth in me, which let me see my inward state and condition towards God. The light, which before had shone in my darkness, and the darkness could not comprehend it, began now to shine out of darkness, and in some measure discovered to me what it was that had before clouded me and brought that sadness and trouble upon me. And now I saw that although I had been in a great degree preserved from the common immoralities and gross pollutions of the world, yet the spirit of the world had hitherto ruled in me, and led me into pride, flattery, vanity, and superfluity, all which was naught. I found there were many plants growing in me which were not of the heavenly Father's planting, and that all these, of whatever sort or kind they were, or how specious soever they might appear, must be plucked up.

Now was all my former life ripped up, and my sins by degrees were set in order before me. And though they looked not with so black a hue and so deep a dye as those of the lewdest sort of people did, yet I found that all sin (even that which had the fairest or finest show, as well as that which was more coarse and foul) brought guilt, and with and for guilt, condemnation on the soul that sinned. This I felt, and was greatly bowed down under the sense thereof.

Now also did I receive a new law—an inward law superadded to the outward—the law of the spirit of life in Christ Jesus, which wrought in me against all evil, not only in deed and in word, but even in thought also; so that everything was brought to judgment, and judgment passed upon all. So that I could not any longer go on in my former ways and course of life, for when I did, judgment took hold upon me for it.

Thus the Lord was graciously pleased to deal with me in somewhat like manner as he had dealt with his people Israel of old when they had transgressed his righteous law, whom by his prophet he called back, required to put away the evil of their doings, bidding them first cease to do evil, then learn to do well, before he would admit them to reason with him, and before he would impart to them the effects of his free mercy. (Isaiah i. 16, 17.)

I was now required by this inward and spiritual law (the law of the spirit of life in Christ Jesus) to put away the evil of my doings, and to cease to do evil; and what in particular the evil was which I was required to put away and to cease from, that measure of the divine light which was now manifested in me discovered to me, and what the light made manifest to be evil, judgment passed upon.

So that here began to be a way cast up before me for me to walk in— a direct and plain way, so plain that a wayfaring man, how weak and simple soever (though a fool to the wisdom and in the judgment of the world) could not err while he continued to walk in it, the error coming in by his going out of it. And this way with respect to me I saw was that measure of divine light which was manifested in me, by which the evil of my doings which I was to put away and to cease from was discovered to me.

By this divine light, then, I saw that though I had not the evil of the common uncleanness, debauchery, profaneness, and pollutions of the world to put away, because I had, through the great goodness of God and a civil education, been preserved out of those grosser evils, yet I had many other evils to put away and to cease from; some of which were not by the world, which lies in wickedness (1 John v. 19), accounted evils; but by the light of Christ were made manifest to me to be evils, and as such condemned in me.

As particularly those fruits and effects of pride that discover themselves in the vanity and superfluity of apparel; which I, as far as my ability would extend to, took, alas! too much delight in. This evil of my doings I was required to put away and cease from; and judgment lay upon me till I did so. Wherefore, in obedience to the inward law, which agreed with the outward (1 Tim. ii. 9; 1 Pet. iii. 3; 1 Tim. vi. 8; James i. 21), I took off from my apparel those unnecessary trimmings of lace, ribbons, and useless buttons, which had no real service, but were set on only for that which was by mistake called ornament; and I ceased to wear rings.

Again, the giving of flattering titles to men between whom and me there was not any relation to which such titles could be pretended to belong. This was an evil I had been much addicted to, and was accounted a ready artist in; therefore this evil also was I required to put away and cease from. So that thenceforward I durst not say, Sir, Master, My Lord, Madam (or My Dame); or say Your Servant to any one to whom I did not stand in the real relation of a servant, which I had never done to any.

Again, respect of persons, in uncovering the head and bowing the knee or body in salutation, was a practice I had been much in the use of; and this, being one of the vain customs of the world, introduced by the spirit of the world, instead of the true honour which this is a false representation of, and used in deceit as a token of respect by persons one to another, who bear no real respect one to another; and besides, this being a type and proper emblem of that divine honour which all ought to pay to Almighty God, and which all of all sorts, who take upon them the Christian name, appear in when they offer their prayers to Him, and therefore should not be given to men;—I found this to be one of those evils which I had been too long doing; therefore I was now required to put it away and cease from it.

Again, the corrupt and unsound form of speaking in the plural number to a single person, *you* to one, instead of *thou*, contrary to the pure, plain, and single language of truth, *thou* to one, and *you* to more than one, which had always been used by God to men, and men to God, as well as one to another, from the oldest record of time till corrupt men, for corrupt ends, in later and corrupt times, to flatter, fawn, and work upon the corrupt nature in men, brought in that false and senseless way of speaking *you* to one, which has since corrupted the modern languages, and hath greatly debased the spirits and depraved the manners of men;—this evil custom I had been as forward in as others, and this I was now called out of and required to cease from.

These and many more evil customs which had sprung up in the night of darkness and general apostacy from the truth and true religion, were now, by the inshining of this pure ray of divine light in my conscience, gradually discovered to me to be what I ought to cease from, shun, and stand a witness against.

But so subtly and withal so powerfully did the enemy work upon the weak part in me, as to persuade me that in these things I ought to make a difference between my father and all other men; and that therefore, though I did disuse these tokens of respect to others, yet I ought still to use them towards him, as he was my father. And so far did this wile of his prevail upon me, through a fear lest I should do amiss in withdrawing any sort of respect or honour from my father which was due unto him, that being thereby beguiled, I continued for a while to demean myself in the same manner towards him, with respect both to language and gesture, as I had always done before. And so long as I did so (standing bare before him, and giving him the accustomed language) he did not express—whatever he thought—any dislike of me.

But as to myself and the work begun in me, I found it was not enough for me to cease to do evil, though that was a good and a great step. I had another lesson before me, which was to learn to do well; which I could by no means do till I had given up with full purpose of mind to cease from doing evil.

And when I had done that, the enemy took advantage of my weakness to mislead me again.

For whereas I ought to have waited in the light for direction and guidance into and in the way of well–doing, and not to have moved till the divine Spirit (a manifestation of which the Lord has been pleased to give unto me for me to profit with or by), the enemy, transforming himself into the appearance of an angel of light, offered himself in that appearance to be my guide and leader into the performance of religious exercises. And I not then knowing the wiles of Satan, and being eager to be doing some acceptable service to God, too readily yielded myself to the conduct of my enemy instead of my friend.

He thereupon, humouring the warmth and zeal of my spirit, put me upon religious performances in my own will, in my own time, and in my own strength; which in themselves were good, and would have been profitable unto me and acceptable unto the Lord, if they had been performed in His will, in His time, and in the ability which He gives. But being wrought in the will of man and at the prompting of the evil one, no wonder that it did me hurt instead of good.

I read abundantly in the Bible, and would set myself tasks in reading, enjoining myself to read so many chapters, sometimes a whole book or long epistle, at a time. And I thought that time well spent, though I was not much the wiser for what I had read, reading it too cursorily, and without the true Guide, the Holy Spirit, which alone could open the understanding and give the true sense of what was read.

I prayed often, and drew out my prayers to a great length, and appointed unto myself certain set times to pray at, and a certain number of prayers to say in a day: we knew not meanwhile what true prayer was, which stands not in words, though the words which are uttered in the movings of the Holy Spirit are very available, but in the breathing of the soul to the heavenly Father through the operation of the Holy Spirit, who maketh intercession sometimes in words and sometimes with sighs and groans only, which the Lord vouchsafes to hear and answer.

This will-worship, which all is that is performed in the will of man and not in the movings of the Holy Spirit, was a great hurt to me, and hindrance of my spiritual growth in the way of truth. But my heavenly Father, who knew the sincerity of my soul to Him and the hearty desire I had to serve Him, had compassion on me, and in due time was graciously pleased to illuminate my understanding further, and to open in me an eye to discern the false spirit, and its way of working from the true, and to reject the former and cleave to the latter.

But though the enemy had by his subtlety gained such advantages over me, yet I went on notwithstanding, and firmly persisted in my godly resolution of ceasing from and denying those things which I was now convinced in my conscience were evil. And on this account a great trial came quickly on me; for the general Quarter Sessions for the Peace coming on, my father, willing to excuse himself from a dirty journey, commanded me to get up betimes and go to Oxford, and deliver in the recognisances he had taken, and bring him an account what justices were on the bench, and what principal pleas were before them; which he knew I knew how to do, having often attended him on those services.

I, who knew how it stood with me better than he did, felt a weight come over me as soon as he had spoken the word; for I presently saw it would bring a very great exercise upon me. But having never resisted his will in anything that was lawful, as this was, I attempted not to make any excuse, but ordering a horse to be ready for me early in the morning, I went to bed, having great strugglings in my breast.

For the enemy came in upon me like a flood, and set many difficulties before me, swelling them up to the highest pitch, by representing them as mountains which I should never be able to get over; and alas! that faith which could remove such mountains, and cast them into the sea, was but very small and weak in me.

He cast into my mind not only how I should behave myself in court and dispatch the business I was sent about, but how I should demean myself towards my acquaintance, of which I had many in that city, with whom I was wont to be jolly; whereas now I could not put off my hat, nor bow to any of them, nor give them their honorary titles (as they are called), nor use the corrupt language of *you* to any one of them, but must keep to the plain and true language of *thou* and *thee*.

Much of this nature revolved in my mind, thrown in by the enemy to discourage and cast me down. And I had none to have recourse to for counsel or help, but to the Lord alone; to whom therefore I poured forth my supplications, with earnest cries and breathings of soul, that He, in whom all power was, would enable me to go through this great exercise, and keep me faithful to Himself therein. And after some time He was pleased to compose my mind to stillness, and I went to rest.

Early next morning I got up, and found my spirit pretty calm and quiet, yet not without a fear upon me lest I should slip and let fall the testimony which I had to bear. And as I rode a frequent cry ran through me to the Lord, in this wise: "Oh, my God, preserve me faithful, whatever befalls me: suffer me not to be drawn into evil, how much scorn and contempt soever may be cast upon me."

Thus was my spirit exercised on the way almost continually; and when I was come within a mile or two of the city, whom should I meet upon the way coming from thence but Edward Burrough. I rode in a montero–cap (a dress more used then than now), and so did he; and because the weather was exceedingly sharp, we both had drawn our caps down, to shelter our faces from the cold, and by that means neither of us knew the other, but passed by without taking notice one of the other; till a few days after, meeting again, and observing each other's dress, we recollected where we had so lately met. Then thought I with myself, oh, how glad should I have been of a word of encouragement and counsel from him when I was under that weighty exercise of mind! But the Lord saw it was not good for me, that my reliance might be wholly upon Him, and not on man.

When I had set up my horse I went directly to the hall where the sessions were held, where I had been but a very little while before a knot of my old acquaintances, espying me, came to me. One of these was a scholar in his gown, another a surgeon of that city (both my school–fellows and fellow–boarders at Thame school), and the third a country gentleman with whom I had long been very familiar.

When they were come up to me they all saluted me after the usual manner, pulling off their hats and bowing, and saying, "Your humble servant, sir," expecting no doubt the like from me. But when they saw me stand still, not moving my cap, nor bowing my knee in way of congee to them, they were amazed, and looked first one upon another, then upon me, and then one upon another again, for a while, without speaking a word.

At length the surgeon, a brisk young man, who stood nearest to me, clapping his hand in a familiar way upon my shoulder, and smiling on me, said, "What, Tom! a Quaker?" To which I readily and cheerfully answered, "Yes, a Quaker." And as the words passed out of my mouth I felt joy spring in my heart; for I rejoiced that I had not been drawn out by them into a compliance with them, and that I had strength and boldness given me to confess myself to be one of that despised people.

They stayed not long with me nor said any more, that I remember to me; but looking somewhat confusedly one upon another, after a while took their leave of me, going off in the same ceremonious manner as they came on.

After they were gone I walked a while about the hall, and went up nearer to the court, to observe both what justices were on the bench and what business they had before them. And I went in fear, not of what they could or would have done to me if they should have taken notice of me, but lest I should be surprised, and drawn unwarily into that which I was to keep out of.

It was not long before the court adjourned to go to dinner, and that time I took to go to the Clerk of the Peace at his house, whom I was well acquainted with. So soon as I came into the room where he was he came and met me, and saluted me after his manner; for he had a great respect for my father and a kind regard for me. And though he was at first somewhat startled at my carriage and language, yet he treated me very civilly, without any reflection or show of lightness. I delivered him the recognisances which my father had sent, and having done the business I came upon, withdrew, and went to my inn to refresh myself, and then to return home.

But when I was ready to take horse, looking out into the street, I saw two or three justices standing just in the way where I was to ride. This brought a fresh concern upon me. I knew if they saw me they would know me; and I concluded, if they knew me, they would stop me and inquire after my father, and I doubted how I should come off with them.

This doubting brought weakness on me, and that weakness led to contrivance how I might avoid this trial. I knew the city pretty well, and remembered there was a back way, which though somewhat about, would bring me out of town without passing by those justices; yet loth I was to go that way. Wherefore I stayed a pretty time, in hopes they would have parted company, or removed to some other place out of my way. But when I had waited until I was uneasy for losing so much time, having entered into reasonings with flesh and blood, the weakness prevailed over me, and away I went the back way, which brought trouble and grief upon my spirit for having shunned the cross.

But the Lord looked on me with a tender eye, and seeing my heart was right to Him, and that what I had done was merely through weakness and fear of falling, and that I was sensible of my failing therein, and sorry for it, He was graciously pleased to pass it by, and speak peace to me again. So that before I got home, as when I went in the morning, my heart was full of breathing prayer to the Lord, that He would vouchsafe to be with me, and uphold and carry me through that day's exercise; so now at my return in the evening, my heart was full of thankful acknowledgments and praises unto Him for His great goodness and favour to me, in having thus far preserved and kept me from falling into anything that might have brought dishonour to His holy name, which I had now taken on me.

But notwithstanding that it was thus with me, and that I found peace and acceptance with the Lord in some good degree, according to my obedience to the convictions I had received by His holy Spirit in me, yet was not the veil so done away, or fully rent, but that there still remained a cloud upon my understanding with respect to my carriage towards my father. And that notion which the enemy had brought into my mind, that I ought to put such a difference between him and all others as that, on account of the paternal relation, I should still deport myself towards him, both in gesture and language, as I had always heretofore done, did yet prevail with me. So that when I came home I went to my father bareheaded, as I used to do, and gave him a particular account of the business he had given me in command, in such manner that we, observing no alteration in my carriage towards him, found no cause to take offence at me.

I had felt for some time before an earnest desire of mind to go again to Isaac Penington's, and I began to question whether, when my father should come (as I concluded ere long he would) to understand I inclined to settle among the people called Quakers, he would permit me the command of his horses, as before. Wherefore, in the morning when I went

24

to Oxford I gave directions to a servant of his to go that day to a gentleman of my acquaintance, who I knew had a riding nag to put off either by sale or to be kept for his work, and desired him, in my name, to send him to me; which he did, and I found him in the stable when I came home.

On this nag I designed to ride next day to Isaac Penington's, and in order thereunto arose betimes and got myself ready for the journey; but because I would pay all due respect to my father, and not go without his consent, or knowledge at the least, I sent one up to him (for he was not yet stirring) to acquaint him that I had a purpose to go to Isaac Penington's, and desired to know if he pleased to command me any service to them. He sent me word he would speak with me before I went, and would have me come up to him, which I did, and stood by his bedside.

Then, in a mild and gentle tone, he said: "I understand you have a mind to go to Mr. Penington's." I answered, "I have so."—"Why," said he, "I wonder why you should. You were there, you know, but a few days ago, and unless you had business with them, don't you think it will look oddly?"—I said, "I thought not."—"I doubt," said he, "you'll tire them with your company, and make them think they shall be troubled with you."—"If," replied I, "I find anything of that, I'll make the shorter stay."—"But," said he, "can you propose any sort of business with them, more than a mere visit?"—"Yes," said I, "I propose to myself not only to see them, but to have some discourse with them."— "Why," said he, in a tone a little harsher, "I hope you don't incline to be of their way."—"Truly," answered I, "I like them and their way very well, so far as I yet understand it; and I am willing to go to them that I may understand it better."

Thereupon he began to reckon up a beadroll of faults against the Quakers, telling me they were a rude, unmannerly people, that would not give civil respect or honour to their superiors, no not to magistrates; that they held many dangerous principles; that they were an immodest shameless people; and that one of them stripped himself stark naked, and went in that unseemly manner about the streets, at fairs and on market days, in great towns.

To all the other charges I answered only, "That perhaps they might be either misreported or misunderstood, as the best of people had sometimes been." But to the last charge of going naked, a particular answer, by way of instance, was just then brought into my mind and put into my mouth, which I had not thought of before, and that was the example of

Isaiah, who went naked among the people for a long time (Isaiah xx. 4). "Ay," said my father, "but you must consider that he was a prophet of the Lord, and had an express command from God to go so."

"Yes, sir," replied I, "I do consider that; but I consider also, that the Jews, among whom he lived, did not own him for a prophet, nor believe that he had such a command from God. And," added I, "how know we but that this Quaker may be a prophet too, and might be commanded to do as he did, for some reason which we understand not?"

This put my father to a stand; so that, letting fall his charges against the Quakers, he only said, "I would wish you not to go so soon, but take a little time to consider of it; you may visit Mr. Penington hereafter."—"Nay, sir," replied I, "pray don't hinder my going now, for I have so strong a desire to go that I do not well know how to forbear." And as I spoke those words, I withdrew gently to the chamber door, and then hastening down stairs, went immediately to the stable, where finding my horse ready bridled, I forthwith mounted, and went off, lest I should receive a countermand.

This discourse with my father had cast me somewhat back in my journey, and it being fifteen long miles thither, the ways bad, and my nag but small, it was in the afternoon that I got thither. And understanding by the servant that took my horse that there was then a meeting in the house (as there was weekly on that day, which was the fourth day of the week, though till then I understood it not), I hastened in, and knowing the rooms, went directly to the little parlour, where I found a few friends sitting together in silence, and I sat down among them well satisfied, though without words.

When the meeting was ended, and those of the company who were strangers withdrawn, I addressed myself to Isaac Penington and his wife, who received me courteously; but not knowing what exercise I had been in, and yet was under, nor having heard anything of me since I had been there before in another garb, were not forward at first to lay sudden hands on me, which I observed, and did not dislike. But as they came to see a change in me, not in habit only, but in gesture, speech, and carriage, and, which was more, in countenance also (for the exercise I had passed through, and yet was under, had imprinted a visible character of gravity upon my face), they were exceedingly kind and tender towards me.

There was then in the family a friend, whose name was Anne Curtis, the wife of Thomas Curtis, of Reading, who was come upon a visit to them, and particularly to see Mary Penington's daughter Guli, who had been ill of the small-pox since I had been there before. Betwixt Mary Penington and this friend I observed some private discourse and whisperings, and I had an apprehension that it was upon something that concerned me. Wherefore I took the freedom to ask Mary Penington if my coming thither had occasioned any inconvenience in the family. She asked me if I had had the small-pox; I told her no. She then told me her daughter had newly had them, and though she was well recovered of them, she had not as yet been down amongst them, but intended to have come down and sat with them in the parlour that evening, yet would rather forbear till another time, than endanger me; and that that was the matter they had been discoursing of. I assured her that I had always been, and then more especially was, free from any apprehension of danger in that respect, and therefore entreated that her daughter might come down. And although they were somewhat unwilling to yield to it, in regard to me, yet my importunity prevailed, and after supper she did come down and sit with us; and though the marks of the distemper were fresh upon her, yet they made no impression upon me, faith keeping out fear.

We spent much of the evening in retiredness of mind, our spirits being weightily gathered inward, so that not much discourse passed among us; neither they to me, nor I to them offered any occasion. Yet I had good satisfaction in that stillness, feeling my spirit drawn near to the Lord, and to them therein.

Before I went to bed they let me know that there was to be a meeting at Wycombe next day, and that some of the family would go to it. I was very glad of it, for I greatly desired to go to meetings, and this fell very aptly, it being in my way home. Next morning Isaac Penington himself went, having Anne Curtis with him, and I accompanied them.

At Wycombe we met with Edward Burrough, who came from Oxford thither that day that I, going thither, met him on the way; and having both our monter-caps on, we recollected that we had met, and passed by each other on the road unknown.

This was a monthly meeting, consisting of friends chiefly, who gathered to it from several parts of the country thereabouts, so that it was pretty large, and was held in a fair room in Jeremiah Stevens' house; the room where I had been at a meeting before, in John Raunce's house, being too little to receive us.

A very good meeting was this in itself and to me. Edward Burrough's ministry came forth among us in life and power, and the assembly was covered therewith. I also, according to my small capacity, had a share therein; for I felt some of that divine power working my spirit into a great tenderness, and not only confirming me in the course I had already entered, and strengthening me to go on therein, but rending also the veil somewhat further, and clearing my understanding in some other things which I had not seen before. For the Lord was pleased to make His discoveries to me by degrees, that the sight of too great a work, and too many enemies to encounter with at once, might not discourage me and make me faint.

When the meeting was ended, the friends of the town taking notice that I was the man that had been at their meeting the week before, whom they then did not know, some of them came and spoke lovingly to me, and would have had me stay with them; but Edward Burrough going home with Isaac Penington, he invited me to go back with him, which I willingly consented to, for the love I had more particularly to Edward Burrough, through whose ministry I had received the first awakening stroke, drew me to desire his company; and so away we rode together.

But I was somewhat disappointed of my expectation, for I hoped he would have given me both opportunity and encouragement to have opened myself to him, and to have poured forth my complaints, fears, doubts, and questionings into his bosom. But he, being sensible that I was truly reached, and that the witness of God was raised and the work of God rightly begun in me, chose to leave me to the guidance of the good Spirit in myself (the Counsellor that could resolve all doubts), that I might not have any dependence on man. Wherefore, although he was naturally of an open and free temper and carriage, and was afterwards always very familiar and affectionately kind to me, yet at this time he kept himself somewhat reserved, and showed only common kindness to me.

Next day we parted, he for London, I for home, under a very great weight and exercise upon my spirit. For I now saw, in and by the farther openings of the Divine light in me, that the enemy, by his false reasonings, had beguiled and misled me with respect to my carriage towards my father. For I now clearly saw that the honour due to parents did not consist in uncovering the head and bowing the body to them, but in a ready obedience to their lawful commands, and in performing all needful services unto them. Wherefore, as I was greatly troubled for what I already had done in that case, though it was through ignorance, so I plainly felt I could no longer continue therein without drawing upon myself the guilt of wilful disobedience, which I well knew would draw after it divine displeasure and judgment.

Hereupon the enemy assaulted me afresh, setting before me the danger I should run myself into of provoking my father to use severity towards me; and perhaps to be casting me utterly off. But over this temptation the Lord, who I cried unto, supported me, and gave me faith to believe that He would bear me through whatever might befall me on that account. Wherefore I resolved, in the strength which He should give me to be faithful to his requirings, whatever might come of it.

Thus labouring under various exercises on the way, I at length got home, expecting I should have but a rough reception from my father. But when I came home, I understood my father was from home; wherefore I sat down by the fire in the kitchen, keeping my mind retired to the Lord, with breathings of spirit to Him, that I might be preserved from falling.

After some time I heard the coach drive in, which put me into a little fear, and a sort of shivering came over me. But by that time he was alighted and come in I had pretty well recovered myself; and as soon as I saw him I rose up and advanced a step or two towards him, with my head covered, and said, "Isaac Penington and his wife remember their loves to thee."

He made a stop to hear what I said, and observing that I did not stand bare, and that I used the word *thee* to him, he, with a stern countenance, and tone that spake high displeasure, only said, "I shall talk with you, sir, another time;" and so hastening from me, went into the parlour, and I saw him no more that night.

Though I foresaw there was a storm arising, the apprehension of which was uneasy to me, yet the peace which I felt in my own breast raised in me a return of thanksgiving to the Lord for His gracious supporting hand, which had thus far carried me through this exercise; with humble cries in spirit to Him that He would vouchsafe to stand by me in it to the end, and uphold me, that I might not fall.

My spirit longed to be among friends, and to be at some meeting with them on the first day, which now drew on, this being the sixth-day night. Wherefore I purposed to go to Oxford on the morrow (which was the seventh day of the week), having heard there was a meeting there. Accordingly, having ordered my horse to be made ready betimes, I got up in the morning and made myself ready also. Yet before I would go (that I might be as observant to my father as possibly I could) I desired my sister to go up to him in his chamber, and acquaint him that I had a mind to go to Oxford, and desired to know if he pleased to command me any service there. He bid her tell me he would not have me go till he had spoken with me; and getting up immediately, he hastened down to me before he was quite dressed.

As soon as he saw me standing with my hat on, his passion transporting him, he fell upon me with both his fists, and having by that means somewhat vented his anger, he plucked off my hat and threw it away. Then stepping hastily out to the stable, and seeing my borrowed nag stand ready saddled and bridled, he asked his man whence that horse came; who telling him he fetched it from Mr. Such−an−one's; "Then ride him presently back," said my father, "and tell Mr. —– I desire he will never lend my son a horse again unless he brings a note from me."

The poor fellow, who loved me well, would fain have made excuses and delays; but my father was positive in his command, and so urgent, that he would not let him stay so much as to take his breakfast (though he had five miles to ride), nor would he himself stir from the stable till he had seen the man mounted and gone.

Then coming in, he went up into his chamber to make himself more fully ready, thinking he had me safe enough now my horse was gone; for I took so much delight in riding that I seldom went on foot.

But while he was dressing himself in his chamber I (who understood what had been done), changing my boots for shoes, took another hat, and acquainting my sister, who loved me very well, and whom I could confide in, whither I meant to go, went out privately, and walked away to Wycombe, having seven long miles thither, which yet seemed little and easy to me, from the desire I had to be among friends.

As thus I travelled all alone, under a load of grief, from the sense I had of the opposition and hardship I was to expect from my father, the enemy took advantage to assault me again, casting a doubt into my mind whether I had done well in thus coming away from my father without his leave or knowledge.

I was quiet and peaceable in my spirit before this question was darted into me; but after that, disturbance and trouble seized upon me, so that I was at a stand what to do—whether to go forward or backward.

Fear of offending inclined me to go back, but desire of the meeting, and to be with friends, pressed me to go forward.

I stood still awhile to consider and weigh as well as I could the matter. I was sensibly satisfied that I had not left my father with any intention of undutifulness or disrespect to him, but merely in obedience to that drawing of spirit, which I was persuaded was of the Lord, to join with his people in worshipping Him; and this made me easy.

But then the enemy, to make me uneasy again, objected, "But how could that drawing be of the Lord which drew me to disobey my father?"

I considered thereupon the extent of paternal power, which I found was not wholly arbitrary and unlimited, but had bounds set unto it; so that as in civil matters it was restrained to things lawful, so in spiritual and religious cases it had not a compulsory power over conscience, which ought to be subject to the heavenly Father. And therefore, though obedience to parents be enjoined to children, yet it is with this limitation [*in the Lord*]: "Children, obey your parents in the Lord; for this is right" (1 Pet. vi. 1).

This turned the scale for going forward, and so on I went. And yet I was not wholly free from some fluctuations of mind, from the besettings of the enemy. Wherefore, although I knew that outward signs did not properly belong to the gospel dispensation, yet for my better assurance I did, in fear and great humility, beseech the Lord that he would be pleased so far to condescend to the weakness of his servant as to give me a sign by which I might certainly know whether my way was right before Him or not.

The sign which I asked was, "That if I had done wrong in coming as I did, I might be rejected or but coldly received at the place I was going to; but if this mine undertaking was right in His sight, He would give me favour with them I went to, so that they should receive me with hearty kindness and demonstrations of love." Accordingly, when I came to John Rance's house (which, being so much a stranger to all, I chose to go to, because I understood the meeting was commonly held there), they received me with more than ordinary kindness, especially Frances Rance, John Rance's then wife, who was both a grave and motherly woman, and had a hearty love to truth, and tenderness towards all that in sincerity sought after it. And this so kind reception, confirming me in the belief that my undertaking was approved of by the Lord, gave great satisfaction and ease to my mind; and I was thankful to the Lord therefor.

Thus it fared with me there; but at home it fared otherwise with my father. He, supposing I had betaken myself to my chamber when he took my hat from me, made no inquiry after me till evening came; and then, sitting by the fire and considering that the weather was very cold, he said to my sister, who sat by him: "Go up to your brother's chamber, and call him down; it may be he will sit there else, in a sullen fit, till he has caught cold." "Alas! sir," said she, "he is not in his chamber, nor in the house neither."

At that my farther, starting, said: "Why, where is he then?"—"I know not, sir," said she, "where he is; but I know that when he saw you had sent away his horse he put on shoes, and went out on foot, and I have not seen him since. And indeed, sir," added she, "I don't wonder at his going away, considering how you used him." This put my father into a great fright doubting I was gone quite away; and so great a passion of grief seized on him, that he forebore not to weep, and to cry out aloud, so that the family heard him: "Oh, my son! I shall never see him more; for he is of so bold and resolute a spirit that he will run himself into danger, and so may be thrown into some gaol or other, where he may lie and die before I can hear of him." Then bidding her light him up to his chamber, he went immediately to bed, where he lay restless and groaning, and often bemoaning himself and me, for the greater part of the night.

Next morning my sister sent a man (whom for his love to me she knew she could trust) to give me this account; and though by him she sent me also fresh linen for my use, in case I should go farther or stay out longer, yet she desired me to come home as soon as I could.

This account was very uneasy to me. I was much grieved that I had occasioned so much grief to my father; and I would have returned that evening after the meeting, but the Friends would not permit it, for the meeting would in all likelihood end late, the days being short, and the way was long and dirty. And besides, John Rance told me that he had something on his mind to speak to my father, and that if I would stay till the next day he would go down with me, hoping, perhaps, that while my father was under this sorrow for me he might work some good upon him. Hereupon concluding to stay till the morrow, I dismissed the man with the things he brought, bidding him tell my sister I intended, God willing, to return home to-morrow, and charging him not to let anybody else know that he had seen me, or where he had been.

Next morning John Rance and I set out, and when we were come to the end of the town we agreed that he should go before and knock at the great gate, and I would come a little after, and go in by the back way. He did so; and when a servant came to open the gate he asked if the Justice was at home. She told him, Yes; and desiring him to come in and sit down in the hall, went and acquainted her master that there was one who desired to speak with him. He, supposing it was one that came for justice, went readily into the hall to him; but he was not a little surprised when he found it was a Quaker. Yet not knowing on what account he came, he stayed to hear his business; but when he found it was about me he fell somewhat sharply on him.

In this time I was come by the back way into the kitchen, and hearing my father's voice so loud, I began to doubt things wrought not well; but I was soon assured of that. For my father having quickly enough of a Quaker's company, left John Rance in the hall, and came into the kitchen, where he was more surprised to find me.

The sight of my hat upon my head made him presently forget that I was that son of his whom he had so lately lamented as lost; and his passion of grief turning into anger, he could not contain himself, but running upon me with both his hands, first violently snatched off my hat and threw it away, then giving me some buffets on my head, he said, "Sirrah, get you up to your chamber."

I forthwith went, he following me at the heels, and now and then giving me a whirret on the ear, which, the way to my chamber lying through the hall where John Rance was, he, poor man, might see and be sorry for (as I doubt not but he was), but could not help me.

This was surely an unaccountable thing, that my father should but a day before express so high a sorrow for me, as fearing he should never see me any more, and yet now, so soon as he did see me, should fly upon me with such violence, and that only because I did not put off my hat, which he knew I did not put on in disrespect to him, but upon a religious principle. But as this hat-honour (as it was accounted) was grown to be a great idol, in those times more especially, so the Lord was pleased to engage His servants in a steady testimony against it, what suffering soever was brought upon them for it. And though some who have been called into the Lord's vineyard at later hours, and since the heat of that day hath been much over, may be apt to account this testimony a small thing to suffer so much upon, as some have done, not only to beating, but to fines and long and hard imprisonments; yet they who, in those times were faithfully exercised in and under it, durst not despise the day of small things, as knowing that he who should do so would not be thought worthy to be concerned in higher testimonies.

I had now lost one of my hats, and I had but one more. That therefore I put on, but did not keep it long; for the next time my father saw it on my head he tore it violently from me, and laid it up with the other, I knew not where. Wherefore I put on my montero–cap, which was all I had left to wear on my head, and it was but a very little while that I had that to wear, for as soon as my father came where I was I lost that also. And now I was forced to go bareheaded wherever I had occasion to go, within doors and without.

This was in the eleventh month, called January, and the weather sharp; so that I, who had been bred up more tenderly, took so great a cold in my head that my face and head were much swollen, and my gums had on them boils so sore that I could neither chew meat nor without difficulty swallow liquids. It held long, and I underwent much pain, without much pity except from my poor sister, who did what she could to give me ease; and at length, by frequent applications of figs and stoned raisins roasted, and laid to the boils as hot as I could bear them, they ripened fit for lancing, and soon after sunk; then I had ease.

Now was I laid up as a kind of prisoner for the rest of the winter, having no means to go forth among friends, nor they liberty to come to me. Wherefore I spent the time much in my chamber in waiting on the Lord, and in reading, mostly in the Bible.

But whenever I had occasion to speak to my father, though I had no hat now to offend him, yet my language did as much; for I durst not say "you" to him, but "thou" or "thee," as the occasion required, and then would he be sure to fall on me with his fists.

At one of these times, I remember, when he had beaten me in that manner, he commanded me, as he commonly did at such times, to go to my chamber, which I did, and he followed me to the bottom of the stairs. Being come thither, he gave me a parting blow, and in a very angry tone said: "Sirrah, if ever I hear you say 'thou' or 'thee' to me again, I'll strike your teeth down your throat." I was greatly grieved to hear him say so. And feeling a word rise in my heart unto him, I turned again, and calmly said unto him: "Would it not be just if God should serve thee so, when thou sayest Thou or Thee to

Him?" Though his hand was up, I saw it sink and his countenance fall, and he turned away and left me standing there. But I, notwithstanding, went up into my chamber, and cried unto the Lord, earnestly beseeching Him that He would be pleased to open my father's eyes, that he might see whom he fought against, and for what; and that He would turn his heart.

After this I had a pretty time of rest and quiet from these disturbances, my father not saying anything to me, nor giving me occasion to say anything to him. But I was still under a kind of confinement, unless I would have run about the country bareheaded like a madman, which I did not see it was my place to do. For I found that, although to be abroad and at liberty among my friends would have been more pleasant to me, yet home was at present my proper place, a school in which I was to learn with patience to bear the cross; and I willingly submitted to it. But after some time a fresh storm, more fierce and sharp than any before, arose and fell upon me; the occasion thereof was this: My father, having been in his younger years, more especially while he lived in London, a constant hearer of those who are called Puritan preachers, had stored up a pretty stock of Scripture knowledge, did sometimes (not constantly, nor very often) cause his family to come together on a first day in the evening, and expound a chapter to them, and pray. His family now, as well as his estate, was lessened; for my mother was dead, my brother gone, and my elder sister at London; and having put off his husbandry, he had put off with it most of his servants, so that he had now but one man— and one maid–servant. It so fell out that on a first–day night he bade my sister, who sat with him in the parlour, call in the servants to prayer.

Whether this was done as a trial upon me or no, I know not, but a trial it proved to me; for they, loving me very well and disliking my father's carriage to me, made no haste to go in, but stayed a second summons. This so offended him that when at length they did go in, he, instead of going to prayer, examined them why they came not in when they were first called; and the answer they gave him being such as rather heightened than abated his displeasure, he with an angry tone said: "Call in that fellow" (meaning me, who was left alone in the kitchen), "for he is the cause of all this." They, as they were backward to go in themselves, so were not forward to call me in, fearing the effect of my father's displeasure would fall upon me, as soon it did, for I, hearing what was said, and not staying for the call, went in of myself. And as soon as I was come in, my father discharged his displeasure on me in very sharp and bitter expressions, which drew from me (in the grief of my heart, to see him so transported with passion) these few words:

"They that can pray with such a spirit, let them; for my part, I cannot." With that my father flew upon me with both his fists, and not thinking that sufficient, stepped hastily to the place where his cane stood, and catching that up, laid on me, I thought, with all his strength. And I, being bareheaded, thought his blows must needs have broken my skull had I not laid mine arm over my head to defend it.

His man seeing this, and not able to contain himself, stepped in between us, and laying hold on the cane, by strength of hand held it so fast, that though he attempted not to take it away, yet he withheld my father from striking with it, which did but enrage him the more. I disliked this in the man, and bade him let go the cane and begone, which he immediately did, and turning to be gone, had a blow on his shoulders for his pains, which did not much hurt him.

But now my sister, fearing lest my father should fall upon me again, besought him to forbear, adding: "Indeed, sir, if you strike him any more, I will throw open the casement and cry out murder, for I am afraid you will kill my brother." This stopped his hand, and after some threatening speeches he commanded me to get to my chamber which I did, as I always did whenever he bade me.

Thither, soon after, my sister followed me, to see my arm and dress it, for it was indeed very much bruised and swelled between the wrist and the elbow, and in some places the skin was broken and beaten off. But though it was very sore, and I felt for some time much pain in it, yet I had peace and quietness in my mind, being more grieved for my father than for myself, who I knew had hurt himself more than me.

This was, so far as I remember, the last time that ever my father called his family to prayer; and this was also the last time that he ever fell, so severely at least, upon me.

Soon after this my elder sister, who in all the time of these exercises of mine had been at London, returned home, much troubled to find me a Quaker, a name of reproach and great contempt then, and she, being at London, had received, I suppose, the worst character of them. Yet though she disliked the people, her affectionate regard for me made her rather pity than despise me, and the more when she understood what hard usage I had met with.

The rest of the winter I spent in a lonesome solitary life, having none to converse with, none to unbosom myself unto, none to ask counsel of, none to seek relief from, but the Lord alone, who yet was more than all. And yet the company and society of faithful and judicious friends would, I thought, have been very welcome as well as helpful to me in my spiritual travail, in which I thought I made slow progress, my soul breathing after further attainments, the sense of which drew from me the following lines:

The winter tree
Resembles me,
  Whose sap lies in its root:
The spring draws nigh;
As it, so I
  Shall bud, I hope, and shoot.

At length it pleased the Lord to move Isaac Penington and his wife to make a visit to my father, and see how it fared with me; and very welcome they were to me, whatever they were to him; to whom I doubt not but they would have been more welcome had it not been for me.

They tarried with us all night, and much discourse they had with my father, both about the principles of truth in general, and me in particular, which I was not privy to. But one thing I remember I afterwards heard of, which was this:

When my father and I were at their house some months before, Mary Penington, in some discourse between them, had told him how hardly her husband's father (Alderman Penington) had dealt with him about his hat; which my father (little then thinking that it would, and so soon too, be his own case) did very much censure the alderman for, wondering that so wise a man as he was should take notice of such a trivial thing as the putting off or keeping on a hat; and he spared not to blame him liberally for it.

This gave her a handle to take hold of him by; and having had an ancient acquaintance with him, and he having always had a high opinion of and respect for her, she, who was a woman of great wisdom, of ready speech, and of a well−resolved spirit, did press so close upon him with this home argument, that he was utterly at a loss how to defend himself.

After dinner next day, when they were ready to take coach to return home, she desired my father that, since my company was so little acceptable to him, he would give me leave to go and spend some time with them, where I should be sure to be welcome.

He was very unwilling I should go, and made many objections against it, all which she answered and removed so clearly, that not finding what excuse further to allege, he at length left it to me, and I soon turned the scale for going.

We were come to the coach−side before this was concluded on, and I was ready to step in, when one of my sisters privately put my father in mind that I had never a hat on. That somewhat startled him, for he did not think it fit I should go from home (and that so far and to stay abroad) without a hat. Wherefore he whispered to her to fetch me a hat, and he entertained them with some discourse in the meantime. But as soon as he saw the hat coning he would not stay till it came, lest I should put it on before him, but breaking off his discourse abruptly, took his leave of them, and hastened in before the hat was brought to me.

I had not one penny of money about me, nor indeed elsewhere; for my father, so soon as he saw that I would be a Quaker, took from me both what money I had and everything of value, or that would have made money, as some plate, buttons, rings, &c., pretending that he would keep them for me till I came to myself again, lest I should destroy them.

But as I had no money, so being among my friends I had no need of any, nor ever hankered after it; though once upon a particular occasion I had liked to have wanted it. The case was this:

I had been at Reading, and set out from thence on the first day of the week, in the morning, intending to reach (as in point of time I well might) Isaac Penington's, where the meeting was to be that day; but when I came to Maidenhead, a thoroughfare town on the way, I was stopped by the watch for riding on that day.

The watchman, laying hold on the bridle, told me I must go with him to the constable; and accordingly I, making no resistance, suffered him to lead my horse to the constable's door. When we were come there the constable told me I must go before the warden, who was the chief officer of that town, and bade the watchman bring me on, himself walking before.

Being come to the warden's door, the constable knocked, and desired to speak with Mr. Warden. He thereupon quickly coming to the door the constable said: "Sir, I have brought a man here to you whom the watch took riding through the town." The warden was a budge old man; and I looked somewhat big too, having a good gelding under me, and a good riding–coat on my back, both which my friend Isaac Penington had kindly accommodated me with for that journey.

The warden therefore taking me to be (as the saying is) somebody, put off his hat and made a low congee to me; but when he saw that I sat still, and neither bowed to him nor moved my hat, he gave a start, and said to the constable: "You said you had brought a man, but he don't behave like a man."

I sat still upon my horse and said not a word, but kept my mind retired to the Lord, waiting to see what this would come to.

The warden then began to examine me, asking me whence I came and whither I was going; I told him I came from Reading and was going to Chalfont. He asked me why I did travel on that day; I told him I did not know that it would give any offence barely to ride or to walk on that day, so long as I did not carry or drive any carriage or horses laden with burthens. "Why," said he, "if your business was urgent, did you not take a pass from the mayor of Reading?"—"Because," replied I, "I did not know nor think I should have needed one."—"Well," said he, "I will not talk with you now, because it is time to go to church, but I will examine you further anon." And turning to the constable, "Have him," said he, "to an inn, and bring him before me after dinner."

The naming of an inn put me in mind that such public–houses were places of expense, and I knew I had no money to defray it; wherefore I said to the warden: "Before thou sendest me to an inn, which may occasion some expense, I think it needful to acquaint thee that I have no money."

At that the warden started again, and turning quickly upon me, said: "How! no money! How can that be? You don't look like a man that has no money."—"However I look," said I, "I tell thee the truth, that I have no money; and I tell it to forewarn thee, that thou mayest not bring any charge upon the town."—"I wonder," said he, "what art you have got, that you can travel without money; you can do more, I assure you, than I can."

I making no answer, he went on and said: "Well, well! but if you have no money, you have a good horse under you, and we can distrain him for the charge."—"But," said I, "the horse is not mine."—"No," said he; "but you have a good coat on your back, and that I hope is your own."— "No," said I, "but it is not, for I borrowed both the horse and the coat."

With that the warden, holding up his hands and smiling, said: "Bless me! I never met with such a man as you are before. What! were you set out by the parish?" Then turning to the constable, he said: "Have him to the Greyhound, and bid the people be civil to him." Accordingly, to the Greyhound I was led, my horse set up, and I put into a large room, and some account, I suppose, given of me to the people of the house.

This was new work to me, and what the issue of it would be I could not foresee; but being left there alone, I sat down, and retired in spirit to the Lord, in whom alone my strength and safety were, and begged support of Him; even that He would be pleased to give me wisdom and words to answer the warden when I should come to be examined again before him.

After some time, having pen, ink, and paper about me, I set myself to write what I thought might be proper, if occasion served, to give the warden; and while I was writing, the master of the house, being come home from his worship, sent the tapster to me to invite me to dine with him. I bid him tell his master that I had not any money to pay for my dinner. He sent the man again to tell me I should be welcome to dine with him though I had no money. I desired him to tell his master "that I was very sensible of his civility and kindness in so courteously inviting me to his table, but I had not freedom to eat of his meat unless I could have paid for it." So he went on with his dinner, and I with my writing.

But before I had finished what was on my mind to write, the constable came again, bringing with him his fellow−constable. This was a brisk genteel young man, a shopkeeper in the town, whose name was Cherry. They saluted me very civilly, and told me they were come to have me before the warden. This put an end to my writing, which

I put into my pocket, and went along with them.

Being come to the warden's, he asked me again the same questions he had asked me before; to which I gave him the like answers. Then he told me the penalty I had incurred, which he said was either to pay so much money or lie so many hours in the stocks, and asked me which I would choose; I replied, "I shall not choose either. And," said I, "I have told thee already that I have no money; though if I had, I could not so far acknowledge myself an offender as to pay any. But as to lying in the stocks, I am in thy power, to do unto me what it shall please the Lord to suffer thee."

When he heard that he paused awhile, and then told me, "He considered that I was but a young man, and might not perhaps understand the danger I had brought myself into, and therefore he would not use the severity of the law upon me; but, in hopes that I would be wiser hereafter, he would pass by this offence and discharge me.

Then putting on a countenance of the greatest gravity, he said to me: "But, young man, I would have you know that you have not only broken the law of the land, but the law of God also; and therefore you ought to ask His forgiveness, for you have highly offended Him."—"That," said I, "I would most willingly do if I were sensible that in this case I had offended Him by breaking any law of His."

"Why," said he, "do you question that?"—"Yes truly," said I; "for I do not know that any law of God doth forbid me to ride on this day."

"No!" said he: "that's strange. Where, I wonder, was you bred? You can read, can't you?"—"Yes," said I, "that I can."—"Don't you then read," said he, "the commandment, 'Remember the Sabbath–day to keep it holy. Six days shalt thou labour and do all thy work; but the seventh day is the Sabbath of the Lord; in it thou shalt not do any work.'"— "Yes," replied I, "I have both read it often, and remember it very well. But that command was given to the Jews, not to Christians; and this is not that day, for that was the seventh day, but this is the first."—"How," said he, "do you know the days of the week no better? You had need then be better taught."

Here the younger constable, whose name was Cherry, interposing, said: "Mr. Warden, the gentleman is in the right as to that, for this is the first day of the week, and not the seventh."

This the old warden took in dudgeon, and looking severely on the constable, said: "What! do you take upon you to teach me? I'll have you know I will not be taught by you."—"As you please for that, sir," said the constable; "but I am sure you are mistaken in this point; for Saturday I know is the seventh day, and you know yesterday was Saturday."

This made the warden hot and testy, and put him almost out of all patience, so that I feared it would have come to a downright quarrel betwixt them, for both were confident and neither would yield; and so earnestly were they engaged in the contest, that there was no room for me to put in a word between them.

At length the old man, having talked himself out of wind, stood still awhile as it were to take breath, and then bethinking himself of me, he turned to me and said: "You are discharged, and may take your liberty to go about your occasions."—"But," said I, "I desire my horse may be discharged too, else I know not how to go."—"Ay, ay," said he, "you shall have your horse;" and turning to the other constable, who had not offended him, he said: "Go, see that his horse be delivered to him."

Away thereupon went I with that constable, leaving the old warden and the young constable to compose their difference as they could. Being come to the inn, the constable called for my horse to be brought out; which done, I immediately mounted, and began to set forward. But the hostler, not knowing the condition of my pocket, said modestly to me: "Sir, don't you forget to pay for your horse's standing?"—"No, truly," said I, "I don't forget it; but I have no money to pay it with, and so I told the warden before."—"Well, hold your tongue," said the constable to the hostler; "I'll see you paid." Then opening the gate, they let me out, the constable wishing me a good journey, and through the town I rode without further molestation; though it was as much sabbath, I thought, when I went out as it was when I came in.

A secret joy arose in me as I rode on the way, for that I had been preserved from doing or saying anything which might give the adversaries of truth advantage against it, or the friends of it; and praises sprang in my thankful heart to the Lord, my preserver.

It added also not a little to my joy that I felt the Lord near unto me, by his witness in my heart, to check and warn me; and my spirit was so far subjected to him as readily to take warning, and stop at his check; an instance of both that very morning I had.

For as I rode between Reading and Maidenhead I saw lying in my way the scabbard of a hanger, which, having lost its hook, had slipped off, I suppose, and dropped from the side of the wearer; and it had in it a pair of knives, whose hafts being inlaid with silver, seemed to be of some value. I alighted and took it up, and clapping it between my thigh and the saddle, rode on a little way; but I quickly found it too heavy for me, and the reprover in me soon began to check. The word arose in me, "What hast thou to do with that? Doth it belong to thee?" I felt I had done amiss in taking it; wherefore I turned back to the place where it lay, and laid it down where I found it. And when afterwards I was stopped and seized on at Maidenhead, I saw there was a Providence in not bringing it with me; which, if it should have been found (as it needs must) under my coat when I came to be unhorsed, might have raised some evil suspicion or sinister thoughts concerning me.

The stop I met with at Maidenhead had spent me so much time that when I came to Isaac Penington's the meeting there was half over, which gave them occasion after meeting to inquire of me if anything had befallen me on the way which had caused me to come so late: whereupon I related to them what exercise I had met with, and how the Lord had helped me through it: which when they had heard, they rejoiced with me, and for my sake.

Great was the love and manifold the kindness which I received from these my worthy friends, Isaac and Mary Penington, while I abode in their family. They were indeed as affectionate parents and tender nurses to me in this time of my religious childhood. For besides their weighty and seasonable counsels and exemplary conversations, they furnished me with means to go to the other meetings of Friends in that country, when the meeting was not in their own house. And indeed, the time I stayed with them was so well spent, that it not only yielded great satisfaction to my mind but turned in good measure to my spiritual advantage in the truth.

But that I might not, on the one hand, bear too hard upon my friends, nor on the other hand forget the house of thraldom, after I had staid with them some six or seven weeks (from the time called Easter to the time called Whitsuntide) I took my leave of them to depart home, intending to walk to Wycombe in one day, and from thence home in another.

That day that I came home I did not see my father, nor until noon the next day, when I went into the parlour, where he was, to take my usual place at dinner.

As soon as I came in I observed by my father's countenance that my hat was still an offence to him; but when I was sat down, and before I had eaten anything, he made me understand it more fully by saying to me, but in a milder tone than he had formerly used to speak to me in, "If you cannot content yourself to come to dinner without your hive on your head (so he called my hat), pray rise, and go take your dinner somewhere else."

Upon these words I arose from the table, and leaving the room went into the kitchen, where I stayed till the servants went to dinner, and then sat down very contentedly with them. Yet I suppose my father might intend that I should have gone into some other room, and there have eaten by myself but I chose rather to eat with the servants, and did so from thenceforward so long as he and I lived together. And from this time he rather chose, as I thought, to avoid seeing me than to renew the quarrel about my hat.

My sisters, meanwhile observing my weariness in words and behaviour, and being satisfied, I suppose, that I acted upon a principle of religion and conscience, carried themselves very kindly to me, and did what they could to mitigate my father's displeasure against me. So that I now enjoyed much more quiet at home, and took more liberty to go abroad amongst my friends, than I had done or could do before. And having informed myself where any meetings of Friends were holden, within a reasonable distance from me, I resorted to them.

At first I went to a town called Hoddenham, in Buckinghamshire, five miles from my father's, where, at the house of one Belson, a few who were called Quakers did meet sometimes on a first day of the week; but I found little satisfaction there. Afterwards, upon further inquiry, I understood there was a settled meeting at a little village called Meadle, about four long miles from me, in the house of one John White, which is continued there still; and to that thenceforward I constantly went while I abode in that country, and was able. Many a sore day's travel have I had thither and back again, being commonly in the winter time (how fair soever the weather was overhead) wet up to the ankles at least; yet, through the goodness of the Lord to me, I was preserved in health.

A little meeting also there was on the fourth day of the week at a town called Bledlow (two miles from me), in the house of one Thomas Saunders, who professed the truth; but

44

his wife, whose name was Damaris, did possess it (she being a woman of great sincerity and lively sense), and to that meeting also I usually went.

But though I took this liberty for the service of God, that I might worship Him in the assemblies of His people, yet did I not use it upon other occasions, but spent my time on other days for the most part in my chamber, in retiredness of mind, waiting on the Lord. And the Lord was graciously pleased to visit me, by His quickening spirit and life, so that I came to feel the operation of His power in my heart, working out that which was contrary to His will, and giving me, in measure, dominion over it.

And as my spirit was kept in due subjection to this divine power, I grew into a nearer acquaintance with the Lord; and the Lord vouchsafed to speak unto me in the inward of my soul, and to open my understanding in His fear, to receive counsel from Him; so that I not only at some times heard His voice, but could distinguish His voice from that of the enemy.

As thus I daily waited on the Lord a weighty and unusual exercise came upon me, which bowed my spirit very low before the Lord. I had seen, in the light of the Lord, the horrible guilt of those deceitful priests, of divers sorts and denominations, who made a trade of preaching, and for filthy lucre sake held the people always learning; yet so taught them as that, by their teaching and ministry, they were never able to come to the knowledge, much less to the acknowledgment, of the truth; for as they themselves hated the light, because their own deeds were evil, so by reviling, reproaching, and blaspheming the true light, wherewith every man that cometh into the world is enlightened (John i. 9), they begat in the people a disesteem of the light, and laboured as much as in them lay to keep their hearers in the darkness, that they might not be turned to the light in themselves, lest by the light they should discover the wickedness of these their deceitful teachers, and turn from them.

Against this practice of these false teachers the zeal of the Lord had flamed in my breast for some time; and now the burthen of the word of the Lord against them fell heavily upon me, with command to proclaim his controversy against them.

Fain would I have been excused from this service, which I judged too heavy for me; wherefore I besought the Lord to take this weight from off me, who was in every respect but young, and lay it upon some other of His servants, of whom he had many, who were much more able and fit for it. But the Lord would not be entreated, but continued the burden upon me with greater weight; requiring obedience from me, and promising to assist me therein. Whereupon I arose from my bed, and in the fear and dread of the Lord committed to writing what He, in the motion of His divine Spirit, dictated to me to write. When I had done it, though the sharpness of the message therein delivered was hard to my nature to be the publisher of, yet I found acceptance with the Lord in my obedience to His will, and His peace filled my heart. As soon as I could I communicated to my friends what I had written; and it was printed in the year 1660, in one sheet of paper, under the title of "An Alarm to the Priests; or, A Message from Heaven to Forewarn them," &c.

Some time after the publishing of this paper, having occasion to go to London, I went to visit George Fox the younger, who with another Friend was then a prisoner in a messenger's hands. I had never seen him, nor he me before; yet this paper lying on the table before him, he, pointing to it, asked me if I was the person that wrote it. I told him I was. "It's much," said the other Friend, "that they bear it." "It is," replied he, "their portion, and they must bear it."

While I was then in London I went to a little meeting of Friends which was then held in the house of one Humphrey Bache, a goldsmith, at the sign of the Snail, in Tower Street. It was then a very troublesome time, not from the government, but from the rabble of boys and rude people, who upon the turn of the time (at the return of the King) took liberty to be very abusive.

When the meeting ended, a pretty number of these unruly folk were got together at the door, ready to receive the Friends as they came forth, not only with evil words, but with blows; which I saw they bestowed freely on some of them that were gone out before me, and expected I should have my share of when I came amongst them. But, quite contrary to my expectation, when I came out, they said one to another, "Let him alone; don't meddle with him; he is no Quaker, I'll warrant you."

This struck me, and was worse to me than if they had laid their fists on me, as they did on others. I was troubled to think what the matter was, or what these rude people saw in me that made them not take me for a Quaker. And upon a close examination of myself, with respect to my habit and deportment, I could not find anything to place it on, but that I had then on my head a large montero-cap of black velvet, the skirt of which being turned up in folds, looked, it seems, somewhat above the then common garb of a Quaker; and this put me out of conceit with my cap.

I came at this time to London from Isaac Penington's, and thither I went again in my way home; and while I stayed there, amongst other Friends who came thither, Thomas Loe, of Oxford, was one. A faithful and diligent labourer he was in the work of the Lord, and an excellent ministerial gift he had. And I, in my zeal for truth, being very desirous that my neighbours might have the opportunity of hearing the gospel, the glad tidings of salvation, livingly and powerfully preached among them, entered into communication with him about it; offering to procure some convenient place in the town where I lived for a meeting to be held, and to invite my neighbours to it, if he could give me any ground to expect his company at it. He told me he was not at his own command, but at the Lord's, and he knew not how He might dispose of him; but wished me, if I found when I was come home that the thing continued with weight upon my mind, and that I could get a fit place for a meeting, I would advertise him of it by a few lines directed to him in Oxford, whither he was then going, and he might then let me know how his freedom stood in that matter.

When therefore I was come home, and had treated with a neighbour for a place to have a meeting in, I wrote to my friend Thomas Loe, to acquaint him that I had procured a place for a meeting, and would invite company to it, if he would fix the time, and give me some ground to hope that he would be at it.

This letter I sent by a neighbour to Thame to be given to a dyer of Oxford, who constantly kept Thame market, with whom I was pretty well acquainted, having sometimes formerly used him not only in his way of trade, but to carry letters between my brother and me when he was a student in that University, for which he was always paid; and had been so careful in the delivery that our letters had always gone safe until now. But this time (Providence so ordering, or at least for my trial permitting it) this letter of mine, instead of being delivered according to its direction, was seized and carried, as I was told, to the Lord Faulkland, who was then called Lord Lieutenant of that county.

The occasion of this stopping of letters at that time was that mad prank of those infatuated fifth–monarchy men, who from their meeting–house in Coleman Street, London, breaking forth in arms, under the command of their chieftain Venner, made an insurrection in the city, on pretence of setting up the kingdom of Jesus, who, it is said, they expected would come down from heaven to be their leader; so little understood they the nature of his kingdom, though he himself had declared it was not of this world.

The King, a little before his arrival in England, had by his declaration from Breda given assurance of liberty to tender consciences, and that no man should be disquieted or called in question for difference of opinion in matters of religion which do not disturb the peace of the kingdom. Upon this assurance dissenters of all sorts relied, and held themselves secure. But now, by this frantic action of a few hot-brained men, the King was by some holden discharged from his royal word and promise, in his foregoing declaration publicly given. And hereupon letters were intercepted and broken open, for discovery of suspected plots and designs against the government; and not only dissenters meetings' of all sorts, without distinction, were disturbed, but very many were imprisoned in most parts throughout the nation; and great search there was in all countries for suspected persons, who, if not found at meetings, were fetched in from their own houses.

The Lord Lieutenant (so called) of Oxfordshire had on this occasion taken Thomas Loe and many others of our friends at a meeting, and sent them prisoners to Oxford Castle, just before my letter was brought to his hand, wherein I had invited Thomas Loe to a meeting; and he, putting the worst construction upon it, as if I, a poor simple lad, had intended a seditious meeting, in order to raise rebellion, ordered two of the deputy-lieutenants who lived nearest to me to send a party of horse to fetch me in.

Accordingly, while I wholly ignorant of what had passed at Oxford, was in daily expectation of an agreeable answer to my letter, came a party of horse one morning to my father's gate, and asked for me.

It so fell out that my father was at that time from home, I think in London; whereupon he that commanded the party alighted and came in. My eldest sister, hearing the noise of soldiers, came hastily up into my chamber, and told me there were soldiers below, who inquired for me. I forthwith went down to them, and found the commander was a barber of Thame, and one who had always been my barber till I was a Quaker. His name was Whately, a bold brisk fellow.

I asked him what his business was with me: he told me I must go with him. I demanded to see his warrant: he laid his hand on his sword, and said that was his warrant. I told him though that was not a legal warrant, yet I would not dispute it, but was ready to bear injuries. He told me he could not help it; he was commanded to bring me forthwith before the deputy-lieutenants, and therefore desired me to order a horse to be got ready, because he was in haste. I let him know I had no horse of my own, and would not meddle with any of my father's horses, in his absence especially; and that therefore, if he would have me with him, he must carry me as he could.

He thereupon taking my sister aside, told her he found I was resolute, and his orders were peremptory; wherefore he desired that she would give order for a horse to be made ready for me, for otherwise he should be forced to mount me behind a trooper, which would be very unsuitable for me, and which he was very unwilling to do. She thereupon ordered a horse to be got ready, upon which, when I had taken leave of my sisters, I mounted, and went off, not knowing whither he intended to carry me.

He had orders, it seems, to take some others also in a neighbouring village, whose names he had, but their houses he did not know. Wherefore, as we rode he asked me if I knew such and such men (whom he named) and where they lived; and when he understood that I knew them, he desired me to show him their houses. "No," said I, "I scorn to be an informer against my neighbours, to bring them into trouble." He thereupon, riding to and fro, found by inquiry most of their houses; but, as it happened, found none of them at home, at which I was glad.

At length he brought me to the house of one called Esquire Clark, of Weston, by Thame, who, being afterwards knighted, was called Sir John Clark; a jolly man, too much addicted to drinking in soberer times, but was now grown more licentious that way, as the times did now more favour debauchery. He and I had known one another for some years, though not very intimately, having met sometimes at the Lord Wenman's table.

This Clark was one of the deputy-lieutenants whom I was to be brought before; and he had gotten another thither to join with him in tendering me the oaths, whom I knew only by name and character; he was called Esquire Knowls, of Grays, by Henley, and reputed a man of better morals than the other.

I was brought into the hall, and kept there; and as Quakers were not so common then as they now are (and indeed even yet, the more is the pity, they are not common in that part of the country), I was made a spectacle and gazing-stock to the family, and by divers I was diversely set upon. Some spake to me courteously, with appearance of compassion;

others ruggedly, with evident tokens of wrath and scorn. But though I gave them the hearing of what they said, which I could not well avoid, yet I said little to them; but keeping my mind as well retired as I could, I breathed to the Lord for help and strength from Him, to bear me up and carry me through this trial, that I might not sink under it, or be prevailed on by any means, fair or foul, to do anything that might dishonour or displease my God.

At length came forth the justices themselves (for so they were, as well as lieutenants), and after they had saluted me, they discoursed with me pretty familiarly; and though Clark would sometimes be a little jocular and waggish (which was somewhat natural to him), yet Knowls treated me very civilly, not seeming to take any offence at my not standing bare before him.

And when a young priest, who as I understood was chaplain in the family, took upon him pragmatically to reprove me for standing with my hat on before the magistrates, and snatched my hat from off my head, Knowls, in a pleasant manner, corrected him, telling him that he mistook himself in taking a cap for a hat (for mine was a montero–cap), and bade him give it me again; which he (though unwillingly) doing, I forthwith put it on my head again, and thenceforward none meddled with me about it.

Then they began to examine me, putting divers questions to me relating to the present disturbances in the nation, occasioned by the late foolish insurrection of those frantic fifth–monarchy men. To all which I readily answered, according to the simplicity of my heart and innocency of my hands, for I had neither done nor thought any evil against the government.

But they endeavoured to affright me with threats of danger, telling me (with inuendoes) that for all my pretence of innocency there was high matter against me, which, if I would stand out, would be brought forth, and that under my own hand. I knew not what they meant by this; but I knew my innocency, and kept to it.

At length, when they saw I regarded not their threats in general, they asked me if I knew one Thomas Loe, and had written of late to him. I then remembered my letter, which till then I had not thought of, and thereupon frankly told them that I did both know Thomas Loe and had lately written to him; but that as I knew I had written no hurt, so I did not fear any danger from that letter. They shook their heads, and said, "It was dangerous to write letters to appoint meetings in such troublesome times."

They added, that by appointing a meeting, and endeavouring to gather a concourse of people together, in such a juncture especially as this was, I had rendered myself a dangerous person. And therefore they could do no less than tender me the oaths of allegiance and supremacy, which therefore they required me to take.

I told them if I could take any oath at all, I would take the oath of allegiance, for I owed allegiance to the King; but I durst not take any oath, because my Lord and Master Jesus Christ had commanded me not to swear at all; and if I brake His command I should thereby both dishonour and displease Him.

Hereupon they undertook to reason with me, and used many words to persuade me that that command of Christ related only to common and profane swearing, not to swearing before a magistrate. I heard them, and saw the weakness of their arguing, but did not return them any answer; for I found my present business was not to dispute, but to suffer; and that it was not safe for me, in this my weak and childish state especially, to enter into reasonings with sharp, quick, witty, and learned men, lest I might thereby hurt both the cause of truth, which I was to bear witness to, and myself; therefore I chose rather to be a fool, and let them triumph over me, than by my weakness give them advantage to triumph over the truth. And my spirit being closely exercised in a deep travail towards the Lord, I earnestly begged of Him that He would be pleased to keep me faithful to the testimony He had committed to me, and not suffer me to be taken in any of the snares which the enemy laid for me. And, blessed be His holy name, He heard my cries, and preserved me out of them.

When the justices saw they could not bow me to their wills, they told me they must send me to prison. I told them I was contented to suffer whatsoever the Lord should suffer them to inflict upon me. Whereupon they withdrew into the parlour, to consult together what to do with me, leaving me meanwhile to be gazed on in the hall.

After a pretty long stay they came forth to me again with a great show of kindness, telling me they were very unwilling to send me to gaol, but would be as favourable to me as possibly they could, and that if I would take the oaths, they would pass by all the other matter which they had against me. I told them I knew they could not justly have anything against me, for I had neither done nor intended anything against the government, or against them. And as to the oaths, I assured them that my refusing them was merely matter of conscience to me, and that I durst not take any oath whatsoever, if it were to save my life.

When they heard this they left me again, and went and signed a mittimus to send me to prison at Oxford, and charged one of the troopers that brought me thither, who was one of the newly-raised militia troop, to convey me safe to Oxford. But before we departed they called the trooper aside, and gave him private instructions what he should do with me, which I knew nothing of till I came thither, but expected I should go directly to the castle.

It was almost dark when we took horse, and we had about nine or ten miles to ride, the weather thick and cold (for it was about the beginning of the twelfth month), and I had no boots, being snatched away from home on a sudden, which made me not care to ride very fast. And my guard, who was a tradesman in Thame, having confidence in me that I would not give him the slip, jogged on without heeding how I followed him.

When I was gone about a mile on the way I overtook my father's man, who, without my knowledge, had followed me at a distance to Weston, and waited there abroad in the stables till he understood by some of the servants that I was to go to Oxford; and then ran before, resolving not to leave me till he saw what they would do with me.

I would have had him return home, but he desired me not to send him back, but let him run on until I came to Oxford. I considered that it was a token of the fellow's affectionate kindness to me, and that possibly I might send my horse home by him; and thereupon stopping my horse I bid him, if he would go on, get up behind me. He modestly refused, telling me he could run as fast as I rode. But when I told him if he would not ride he should not go forward, he, rather than leave me, leaped up behind me, and on we went.

But he was not willing I should have gone at all. He had a great cudgel in his hand, and a strong arm to use it; and being a stout fellow, he had a great mind to fight the trooper, and rescue me. Wherefore he desired me to turn my horse and ride off, and if the trooper offered to pursue, leave him to deal with him.

I checked him sharply for that, and charged him to be quiet, and not think hardly of the poor trooper, who could do no other nor less than he did; and who, though he had an ill journey in going with me, carried himself civilly to me. I told him also that I had no need to fly, for I had done nothing that would bring guilt or fear upon me, neither did I go with an ill-will; and this quieted the man. So on we went, but were so far cast behind the trooper, that we had lost both sight and hearing of him, and I was fain to mend my pace to get up to him again.

We came pretty late into Oxford on the seventh day of the week, which was the market day; and, contrary to my expectation (which was to have been carried to the castle), my trooper stopped in the High Street, and calling at a shop asked for the master of the house, who coming to the door, he delivered to him the mittimus, and with it a letter from the deputy-lieutenants (or one of them), which when he had read he asked where the prisoner was. Whereupon the soldier pointing to me, he desired me to alight and come in, which when I did he received me civilly.

The trooper, being discharged of his prisoner, marched back, and my father's man, seeing me settled in better quarters than he expected, mounted my horse and went off with him.

I did not presently understand the quality of my keeper, but I found him a genteel courteous man, by trade a linen-draper; and, as I afterwards understood, he was City Marshal, had a command in the county troop, and was a person of good repute in the place; his name was— Galloway.

Whether I was committed to him out of regard to my father, that I might not be thrust into a common gaol, or out of a politic design to keep me from the conversation of my friends, in hopes that I might be drawn to abandon this profession, which I had but lately taken up, I do not know. But this I know, that though I wanted no civil treatment nor kind accommodations where I was, yet after once I understood that many Friends were prisoners in the castle, and amongst the rest Thomas Loe, I had much rather have been among them there, with all the inconveniences they underwent, than where I was with the best entertainment. But this was my present lot, and therefore with this I endeavoured to be content.

It was quickly known in the city that a Quaker was brought in prisoner, and committed to the Marshal. Whereupon (the men Friends being generally prisoners already in the castle) some of the women Friends came to me to inquire after me, and to visit me; as Silas Norton's wife, and Thomas Loe's wife, who were sisters, and another woman

Friend, who lived in the same street where I was, whose husband was not a Quaker, but kindly affected towards them, a baker by trade, and his name, as I remember,—Ryland.

By some of these an account was soon given to the Friends who were prisoners in the castle of my being taken up and brought prisoner to the Marshal's; whereupon it pleased the Lord to move on the heart of my dear friend Thomas Loe to salute me with a tender and affectionate letter in the following terms:

"MY BELOVED FRIEND,

"In the truth and love of the Lord Jesus, by which life and salvation is revealed in the saints, is my dear love unto thee, and in much tenderness do I salute thee. And, dear heart, a time of trial God hath permitted to come upon us, to try our faith and love to Him; and this will work for the good of them that through patience endure to the end. And I believe God will be glorified through our sufferings, and His name will be exalted in the patience and long–suffering of His chosen. When I heard that thou wast called into this trial, with the servants of the Most High, to give thy testimony to the truth of what we have believed, it came into my heart to write unto thee, and to greet thee with the embraces of the power of an endless life, where our faith stands, and unity is felt with the saints for ever. Well, my dear friend, let us live in the pure counsel of the Lord, and dwell in His strength, which gives us power and sufficiency to endure all things for His name's sake; and then our crown and reward will be with the Lord for ever, and the blessings of His heavenly kingdom will be our portion. Oh, dear heart, let us give up all freely into the will of God, that God may be glorified by us, and we comforted together in the Lord Jesus; which is the desire of my soul, who am thy dear and loving friend in the eternal truth,

"THOMAS LOE.

"We are more than forty here, who suffer innocently for the testimony of a good conscience, because we cannot swear, and break Christ's commands; and we are all well, and the blessing and presence of God is with us. Friends here salute thee. Farewell! The power and the wisdom of the Lord God be with thee. Amen."

Greatly was my spirit refreshed and my heart gladdened, at the reading of this consoling letter from my friend; and my soul blessed the Lord for His love and tender goodness to me in moving His servant to write thus unto me.

But I had cause soon after to double and redouble my thankful acknowledgment to the Lord my God, who put it into the heart of my dear friend Isaac Penington also to visit me with some encouraging lines from Aylesbury Gaol, where he was then a prisoner; and from whence (having heard that I was carried prisoner to Oxford) he thus saluted me:–

"DEAR THOMAS,

"Great hath been the Lord's goodness to thee in calling thee out of that path of vanity and death wherein thou wast running towards destruction; to give thee a living name, and an inheritance of life among His people; which certainly will be the end of thy faith in Him and obedience to Him. And let it not be a light thing in thine eyes that He now accounteth thee worthy to suffer among His choice lambs, that He might make thy crown weightier and thy inheritance the fuller. Oh that that eye and heart may be kept open in thee which knoweth the value of these things, and that thou mayst be kept close to the feelings of the life, that thou mayst be fresh in thy spirit in the midst of thy sufferings, and mayst reap the benefit of them; finding that pared off thereby which hindereth the bubblings of the everlasting springs, and maketh unfit for the breaking forth and enjoyment of the pure power! This is the brief salutation of my dear love to thee, which desireth thy strength and settlement in the power, and the utter weakening of thee as to self. My dear love is to thee, with dear Thomas Goodyare and the rest of imprisoned Friends.

"I remain thine in the truth, to which the Lord my God preserve thee single and faithful.

"I. PENINGTON.

"From Aylesbury Gaol, the 14th of the 12th month, 1660."

Though these epistolary visits in the love of God were very comfortable and confirming to me, and my heart was thankful to the Lord for them, yet I longed after personal conversation with Friends, and it was hard, I thought, that there should be so many faithful servants of God so near me, yet I should not be permitted to come at them, to enjoy their company, and reap both the pleasure and benefit of their sweet society.

For although my Marshal−keeper was very kind to me, and allowed me the liberty of his house, yet he was not willing I should be seen abroad; the rather, perhaps, because he understood I had been pretty well known in that city. Yet once the friendly baker got him to let me step over to his house, and once (and but once) I prevailed with him to let me visit my friends in the castle; but it was with these conditions, that I should not go forth till it was dark, that I would muffle myself up in my cloak, and that I would not stay out late: all which I punctually observed.

When I came thither, though there were many Friends prisoners, I scarce knew one of them by face, except Thomas Loe, whom I had once seen at Isaac Penington's; nor did any of them know me, though they had generally heard that such a young man as I was convinced of the truth, and come among Friends.

Our salutation to each other was very grave and solemn, nor did we entertain one another with much talk, or with common discourses; but most of the little time I had with them was spent in a silent retiredness of spirit, waiting upon the Lord. Yet before we parted we imparted one to another some of the exercises we had gone through; and they seeming willing to understand the ground and manner of my commitment, I gave them a brief account thereof, letting Thomas Loe more particularly know that I had directed a letter to him, which having fallen into the hand of the Lord Lieutenant, was (so far as I could learn) the immediate cause of my being taken up.

Having stayed with them as long as my limited time would permit (which I thought was but very short), that I might keep touch with my keeper and come home in due time, I took leave of my friends there, and with mutual embraces parting, returned to my (in some sense more easy, but in others less easy) prison, where after this I stayed not long before I was brought back to my father's house.

For after my father was come home, who, as I observed before, was from home when I was taken, he applied himself to those justices that had committed me, and not having disobliged them when he was in office, easily obtained to have me sent home, which between him and them was thus contrived.

There was about this time a general muster and training of the militia forces at Oxford, whither on that occasion came the Lord Lieutenant and deputy–lieutenants of the county, of which number they who committed me were two.

When they had been awhile together, and the Marshal with them, he stepped suddenly in, and in haste told me I must get ready quickly to go out of town, and that a soldier would come by and bye to go with me. This said, he hastened to them again, not giving me any intimation how I was to go, or whither.

I needed not much time to get ready in; but I was uneasy in thinking what the Friends of the town would think of this my sudden and private removal; and I feared lest any report should be raised that I had purchased my liberty by an unfaithful compliance. Wherefore I was in care how to speak with some Friends about it; and that friendly baker, whose wife was a Friend, living on the other side of the street at a little distance, I went out at a back door, intending to step over the way to their house, and return immediately.

It so fell out that some of the lieutenants (of whom Esquire Clark, who committed me, was one) were standing in the balcony at a great inn or tavern, just over the place where I was to go by; and he spying me, called out to the soldiers, who stood thick in the street, to stop me. They being generally gentlemen's servants, and many of them knowing me, did civilly forbear to lay hold on me, but calling modestly after me, said, "Stay, sir, stay; pray come back." I heard, but was not willing to hear, therefore rather mended my pace, that I might have got within the door. But he calling earnestly after me, and charging them to stop me, some of them were fain to run, and laying hold on me before I could open the door, brought me back to my place again.

Being thus disappointed, I took a pen and ink, and wrote a few lines, which I sealed up, and gave to the apprentice in the shop, who had carried himself handsomely towards me, and desired him to deliver it to that Friend who was their neighbour, which he promised to do.

By the time I had done this came the soldier that was appointed to conduct me out of town. I knew the man, for he lived within a mile of me, being, through poverty, reduced to keep an alehouse; but he had lived in better fashion, having kept an inn at Thame, and by that means knew how to behave himself civilly, and did so to me.

He told me he was ordered to wait on me to Wheatley, and to tarry there at such an inn, until Esquire Clark came thither, who would then take me home with him in his coach. Accordingly to Wheatley we walked (which is from Oxford some four or five miles), and long we had not been there before Clark and a great company of men came in.

He alighted, and stayed awhile to eat and drink (though he came but from Oxford), and invited me to eat with him; but I, though I had need enough, refused it; for indeed their conversation was a burthen to my life, and made me often think of and pity good Lot.

He seemed, at that time, to be in a sort of mixed temper, between pleasantness and sourness. He would sometimes joke (which was natural to him), and cast out a jesting flirt at me; but he would rail maliciously against the Quakers. "If" said he to me, "the King would authorise me to do it, I would not leave a Quaker alive in England, except you. I would make no more," added he, "to set my pistol to their ears and shoot them through the head, than I would to kill a dog." I told him I was sorry he had so ill an opinion of the Quakers, but I was glad he had no cause for it, and I hoped he would be of a better mind.

I had in my hand a little walking–stick with a head on it, which he commended, and took out of my hand to look at it; but I saw his intention was to search it, whether it had a tuck in it, for he tried to have drawn the head; but when he found it was fast he returned it to me.

He told me I should ride with him to his house in his coach, which was nothing pleasant to me; for I had rather have gone on foot (as bad as the ways were), that I might have been out of his company. Wherefore I took no notice of any kindness in the offer, but only answered I was at his disposal, not mine own.

But when we were ready to go the Marshal came to me, and told me if I pleased I should ride his horse, and he would go in the coach with Mr. Clark. I was glad of the offer, and only told him he should take out his pistols then, for I would not ride with them. He took them out, and laid them in the coach by him, and away we went.

It was a very fine beast that I was set on, by much the best in the company. But though she was very tall, yet the ways being very foul, I found it needful, as soon as I was out of town, to alight and take up the stirrups. Meanwhile, they driving hard on, I was so far behind, that being at length missed by the company, a soldier was sent back to look after me.

As soon as I had fitted my stirrups and was remounted I gave the rein to my mare, which being courageous and nimble, and impatient of delay, made great speed to recover the company; and in a narrow passage the soldier, who was my barber, that had fetched me from home, and I met upon so brisk a gallop that we had enough to do on either side to pull up our horses and avoid a brush.

When we were come to Weston, where Esquire Clark lived, he took the Marshal and some others with him into the parlour; but I was left in the hall, to be exposed a second time for the family to gaze on.

At length himself came out to me, leading in his hand a beloved daughter of his, a young woman of about eighteen years of age, who wanted nothing to have made her comely but gravity. An airy piece she was, and very merry she made herself at me. And when they had made themselves as much sport with me as they would, the Marshal took his leave of them, and mounting me on a horse of Clark's had me home to my father's that night.

Next morning, before the Marshal went away, my father and he consulted together how to entangle me. I felt there were snares laid, but I did not know in what manner or to what end till the Marshal was ready to go. And then, coming where I was to take his leave of me, he desired me to take notice, that although he had brought me home to my father's house again, yet I was not discharged from my imprisonment, but was his prisoner still; and that he had committed me to the care of my father, to see me forthcoming whenever I should be called for. And therefore he expected I should in all things observe my father's orders, and not go out at any time from the house without his leave.

Now I plainly saw the snare, and to what end it was laid; and I asked him if this device was not contrived to keep me from going to meetings; he said I must not go to meetings.

Whereupon I desired him to take notice that I would not own myself a prisoner to any man while I continued here; that if he had power to detain me prisoner, he might take me back again with him if he would, and I should not refuse to go with him. But I bade him assure himself, that while I was at home I would take my liberty both to go to meetings and to visit Friends. He smiled, and said if I would be resolute he could not help it; and so took his leave of me.

By this I perceived that the plot was of my father's laying, to have brought me under such an engagement as should have tied me from going to meetings; and thereupon I expected I should have a new exercise from my father.

It was the constant manner of my father to have all the keys of the out–doors of his house (which were four, and those linked upon a chain) brought up into his chamber every night, and fetched out from thence in the morning; so that none could come in or go out in the night without his knowledge.

I knowing this, suspected that if I got not out before my father came down I should be stopped from going out at all that day. Wherefore (the passage from my chamber lying by his chamber door) I went down softly without my shoes, and as soon as the maid had opened the door I went out (though too early), and walked towards the meeting at Meadle, four long miles off.

I expected tõ have been talked with about it when I came home, but heard nothing of it, my father resolving to watch me better next time.

This I was aware of; and therefore on the next first day I got up early, went down softly, and hid myself in a back room before the maid was stirring.

When she was up she went into my father's chamber for the keys; but he bade her leave them till he was up, and he would bring them down himself; which he did, and tarried in the kitchen, through which he expected I would go.

The manner was, that when the common doors were opened the keys were hung upon a pin in the hall. While therefore my father stayed in the kitchen expecting my coming, I, stepping gently out of the room where I was, reached the keys, and opening another door, not often used, slipped out, and so got away.

I thought I had gone off undiscovered; but whether my father saw me through the window, or by what means he knew of my going, I know not; but I had gone but a little way before I saw him coming after me.

The sight of him put me to a stand in my mind whether I should go on or stop. Had it been in any other case than that of going to a meeting I could not in any wise have gone a step farther. But I considered that the intent of my father's endeavouring to stop me was to hinder me from obeying the call of my heavenly Father, and to stop me from going to worship Him in the assembly of His people; upon this I found it my duty to go on, and observing that my father gained ground upon me, I somewhat mended my pace.

This he observing, mended his pace also, and at length ran. Whereupon I ran also, and a fair course we had through a large meadow of his which lay behind his house and out of sight of the town. He was not, I suppose, then above fifty years of age, and being light of body and nimble of foot, he held me to it for a while. But afterwards slacking his pace to take breath, and observing that I had gotten ground of him, he turned back and went home; and, as I afterwards understood, telling my sisters how I had served him, he said, "Nay, if he will take so much pains to go, let him go if he will." And from that time forward he never attempted to stop me, but left me to my liberty, to go when and whither I would; yet kept me at the usual distance, avoiding the sight of me as much as he could, as not able to bear the sight of my hat on, nor willing to contend with me again about it.

Nor was it long after this before I was left not only to myself, but in a manner by myself; for the time appointed for the coronation of the King (which was the 23rd of the second month, called April) drawing on, my father, taking my two sisters with him, went up to London some time before, that they might be there in readiness, and put themselves into a condition to see so great a solemnity, leaving nobody in the house but myself and a couple of servants. And though this was intended only for a visit on that occasion, yet it proved the breaking of the family; for he bestowed both his daughters there in marriage, and took lodgings for himself, so that afterwards they never returned to settle at Crowell.

Being now at liberty, I walked over to Aylesbury, with some other Friends, to visit my dear friend Isaac Penington, who was still a prisoner there. With him I found dear John Whitehead, and between sixty and seventy more, being well nigh all the men Friends that were then in the county of Bucks; many of them were taken out of their houses by armed men, and sent to prison, as I had been, for refusing to swear. Most of these were thrust into an old room behind the gaol, which had anciently been a malt–house, but was now so decayed that it was scarce fit for a doghouse; and so open it lay, that the prisoners might have gone out at pleasure. But these were purposely put there, in confidence that they would not go out, that there might be room in the prison for others, of other professions and names, whom the gaoler did not trust there.

While this imprisonment lasted, which was for some months, I went afterwards thither sometimes to visit my suffering brethren; and because it was a pretty long way (some eight or nine miles), too far to be walked forward and backward in one day, I sometimes stayed a day or two there, and lay in the malt house among my friends, with whom I delighted to be.

After this imprisonment was over, I went sometimes to Isaac Penington's house at Chalfont, to visit that family, and the Friends thereabouts. There was then a meeting for the most part twice a week in his house; but one first–day in four there was a more general meeting (which was thence called the monthly meeting) to which resorted most of the Friends of other adjacent meetings; and to that I usually went, and sometimes made some stay there.

Here I came acquainted with a friend of London, whose name was Richard Greenaway, by trade a tailor, a very honest man, and one who had received a gift for the ministry.

He having been formerly in other professions of religion, had then been acquainted with one John Ovy, of Watlington, in Oxfordshire, a man of some note among the professors there, and understanding upon inquiry that I knew him, he had some discourse with me about him; the result whereof was, that he, having an intention then shortly to visit some meetings of Friends in this county and the adjoining parts of Oxfordshire and Berkshire, invited me to meet him (upon notice given), and to bear him company in that journey; and in the way bring him to John Ovy's house, with whom I was well acquainted; which I did.

We were kindly received, the man and his wife being very glad to see both their old friend Richard Greenaway and me also, whom they had been very well acquainted with formerly, but had never seen me since I was a Quaker.

Here we tarried that night, and in the evening had a little meeting there with some few of John Ovy's people, amongst whom Richard Greenaway declared the truth; which they attentively heard, and did not oppose, which at that time of day we reckoned was pretty well, for many were apt to cavil.

This visit gave John Ovy an opportunity to inquire of me after Isaac Penington, whose writings (those which he had written before he came among Friends) he had read, and had a great esteem of, and he expressed a desire to see him, that he might have some discourse with him, if he knew how. Whereupon I told him that if he would take the pains to go to his house I would bear him company thither, introduce him, and engage he should have a kind reception.

This pleased him much; and he embracing the offer, I undertook to give him notice of a suitable time, which after I had gone this little journey with my friend Richard Greenaway and was returned, I did, making choice of the monthly meeting to go to.

We met by appointment at Stoken Church, with our staves in our hands, like a couple of pilgrims, intending to walk on foot; and having taken some refreshment and rest at Wycombe, went on cheerfully in the afternoon, entertaining each other with grave and religious discourse, which made the walk the easier, and so reached thither in good time, on the seventh day of the week.

I gave my friends an account who this person was whom I had brought to visit them, and the ground of his visit. He had been a professor of religion from his childhood to his old age (for he was now both grey–headed and elderly), and was a teacher at this time, and had long been so amongst a people, whether Independents or Baptists I do not well remember. And so well thought of he was, for his zeal and honesty, that in those late professing times he was thrust into the Commission of the Peace, and thereby lifted up on the Bench; which neither became him nor he it, for he wanted indeed most of the qualifications requisite for a Justice of the Peace: an estate to defray the charge of the office and to bear him up in a course of living above contempt; a competent knowledge in the laws, and a presence of mind or body, or both, to keep offenders in some awe; in all which he was deficient; for he was but a fellmonger by trade, accustomed to ride upon his pack of skins, and had very little estate, as little knowledge of the law, and of but a mean presence and appearance to look on. But as my father, I suppose, was the means of getting him put into the Commission, so he, I know, did what he could to countenance him in it, and help him through it at every turn, till that turn came (at the King's return) which turned them both out together.

My friends received me in affectionate kindness, and my companion with courteous civility. The evening was spent in common but grave conversation; for it was not a proper season for private discourse, both as we were somewhat weary with our walk, and there were other companies of Friends come into the family, to be at the meeting next day.

But in the morning I took John Ovy into a private walk, in a pleasant grove near the house, whither Isaac Penington came to us; and there in discourse both answered all his questions, objections, and doubts, and opened to him the principles of truth, to his both admiration and present satisfaction. Which done, we went in to take some refreshment before the meeting began.

Of those Friends who were come overnight in order to be at the meeting, there was Isaac's brother, William Penington, a merchant of London, and with him a Friend (whose name I have forgotten), a grocer of Colchester, in Essex; and there was also our friend George Whitehead, whom I had not, that I remember, seen before.

The nation had been in a ferment ever since that mad action of the frantic fifth–monarchy men, and was not yet settled; but storms, like thunder–showers, flew here and there by coast, so that we could not promise ourselves any safety or quiet in our meetings. And though they had escaped disturbance for some little time before, yet so it fell out that a party of horse were appointed to come and break up the meeting that day, though we knew nothing of it till we heard and saw them.

The meeting was scarce fully gathered when they came; but we that were in the family, and many others, were settled in it in great peace and stillness, when on a sudden the prancing of the horses gave notice that a disturbance was at hand.

We all sat still in our places, except my companion John Ovy, who sat next to me. But he being of a profession that approved Peter's advice to his Lord, "to save himself," soon took the alarm, and with the nimbleness of a stripling, cutting a caper over the form that stood before him, ran quickly out at a private door, which he had before observed, which led through the parlour into the gardens, and from thence into an orchard; where he hid himself in a place so obscure, and withal so convenient for his intelligence by observation of what passed, that no one of the family could scarce have found a likelier.

By the time he was got into his burrow came the soldiers in, being a party of the county troop, commanded by Matthew Archdale of Wycombe. He behaved himself civilly, and said he was commanded to break up the meeting, and carry the men before a justice of the peace; but he said he would not take all; and thereupon began to pick and choose, chiefly as his eye guided him, for I suppose he knew very few.

He took Isaac Penington and his brother, George Whitehead, and the Friend of Colchester, and me, with three or four more of the county, who belonged to that meeting.

He was not fond of the work, and that made him take no more; but he must take some, he said, and bade us provide to go with him before Sir William Boyer of Denham, who was a justice of the peace. Isaac Penington being but weakly, rode, but the rest of us walked thither, it being about four miles.

When we came there the Justice carried himself civilly to us all, courteously to Isaac Penington as being a gentleman of his neighbourhood; and there was nothing charged against us but that we were met together without word or deed. Yet this being contrary to a late proclamation, given forth upon the rising of the fifth–monarchy men, whereby all dissenters' meetings were forbidden, the Justice could do no less than take notice of us.

Wherefore he examined all of us whom he did not personally know, asking our names and the places of our respective habitations. But when he had them, and considered from what distant parts of the nation we came, he was amazed; for George Whitehead was of Westmoreland, in the north of England; the grocer was of Essex; I was of Oxfordshire; and William Penington was of London.

Hereupon he told us that our case looked ill, and he was sorry for it: "for how," said he, "can it be imagined that so many could jump altogether at one time and place, from such remote quarters and parts of the kingdom, if it was not by combination and appointment?"

He was answered that we were so far from coming thither by agreement or appointment, that none of us knew of the others' coming, and for the most of us, we had never seen one another before; and that therefore he might impute it to chance, or, if he pleased, to Providence.

He urged upon us that an insurrection had been lately made by armed men, who pretended to be more religious than others; that that insurrection had been plotted and contrived in their meeting–house, where they assembled under colour of worshipping God; that in their meeting–house they hid their arms, and armed themselves, and out of their meeting–house issued forth in arms, and killed many; so that the government could not be safe unless such meetings were suppressed.

We replied, we hoped he would distinguish and make a difference between the guilty and the innocent, and between those who were principled for fighting and those who were principled against it, which we were, and had been always known to be so; that our meetings were public, our doors standing open to all comers, of all ages, sexes, and persuasions, men, women, and children, and those that were not of our religion, as well as those that were; and that it was next to madness for people to plot in such meetings.

He told us we must find sureties for our good behaviour, and to answer our contempt of the King's proclamation at the next general Quarter Sessions, or else he must commit us.

We told him that, knowing our innocency and that we had not misbehaved ourselves, nor did meet in contempt of the King's authority, but purely in obedience to the Lord's requirings to worship Him, which we held ourselves in duty bound to do, we could not consent to be bound, for that would imply guilt which we were free from.

"Then," said he, "I must commit you;" and ordered his clerk to make a mittimus. And divers mittimuses were made, but none of them would hold; for still, when they came to be read, we found such flaws in them as made him throw them aside, and write more.

He had his eye often upon me, for I was a young man, and had at that time a black suit on. At length he bid me follow him, and went into a private room and shut the door upon me.

I knew not what he meant by this; but I cried in spirit to the Lord, that he would be pleased to be a mouth and wisdom to me, and keep me from being entangled in any snare.

He asked me many questions concerning my birth, my education, my acquaintance in Oxfordshire, particularly what men of note I knew there; to all which I gave him brief but plain and true answers, naming several families of the best rank in that part of the county where I dwelt.

He asked me how long I had been of this way, and how I came to be of it. Which when I had given him some account of, he began to persuade me to leave it, and return to the right way—the Church, as he called it. I desired him to spare his pains in that respect, and forbear any discourse of that kind, for that I was fully satisfied the way I was in was the right way, and hoped the Lord would so preserve me in it that nothing should be able to draw or drive me out of it. He seemed not pleased with that, and thereupon went out to the rest of the company, and I followed him, glad in my heart that I had escaped so well, and praising God for my deliverance.

When he had taken his seat again at the upper end of a fair hall, he told us he was not willing to take the utmost rigour of the law against us, but would be as favourable to us as he could. And therefore he would discharge, he said, Mr. Penington himself, because he was but at home in his own house. And he would discharge Mr. Penington of London, because he came but as a relation to visit his brother. And he would discharge the grocer of Colchester, because he came to bear Mr. Penington of London company, and to be acquainted with Mr. Isaac Penington, whom he had never seen before. And as for those others of us who were of this county, he would discharge them, for the present at least, because they being his neighbours, he could send for them when he would. "But as for you," said he to George Whitehead and me, "I can see no business you had there, and therefore I intend to hold you to it, either to give bail or go to gaol."

We told him we could not give bail. "Then," said he, "you must go to gaol;" and thereupon he began to write our mittimus; which puzzled him again; for he had discharged so many, that he was at a loss what to lay as the ground of our commitment, whose case differed nothing in reality from theirs whom he had discharged.

At length, having made divers draughts (which still George Whitehead showed him the defects of), he seemed to be weary of us; and rising up said unto us: "I consider that it is grown late in the day, so that the officer cannot carry you to Aylesbury to-night, and I suppose you will be willing to go back with Mr. Penington; therefore if you will promise to be forthcoming at his house to-morrow morning, I will dismiss you for the present, and you shall hear from me again to–morrow."

We told him we did intend, if he did not otherwise dispose of us, to spend that night with our friend Isaac Penington, and would, if the Lord gave us leave, be there in the morning, ready to answer his requirings. Whereupon he dismissed us all, willing, as we thought, to be rid of us; for he seemed not to be of an ill temper, nor desirous to put us to trouble, if he could help it.

Back then we went to Isaac Penington's. But when we were come thither, oh the work we had with poor John Ovy! He was so dejected in mind, so covered with shame and confusion of face for his cowardliness, that we had enough to do to pacify him towards himself.

The place he had found out to shelter himself in was so commodiously contrived, that undiscovered he could discern when the soldiers went off with us, and understand when the bustle was over and the coast clear. Whereupon he adventured to peep out of his hole, and in a while drew near by degrees to the house again; and finding all things quiet and still, he adventured to step within the doors, and found the Friends who were left behind peaceably settled in the meeting again.

The sight of this smote him, and made him sit down among them. And after the meeting was ended, and the Friends departed to their several homes, addressing himself to Mary Penington, as the mistress of the house, he could not enough magnify the bravery and courage of the Friends, nor sufficiently debase himself. He told her how long he had been a professor, what pains he had taken, what hazards he had run, in his youthful days, to get to meetings; how, when the ways were forelaid and passages stopped, he swam through rivers to reach a meeting; and now, said he, that I am grown old in the profession of religion, and have long been an instructor and encourager of others, that I should thus shamefully fall short myself, is matter of shame and sorrow to me.

Thus he bewailed himself to her. And when we came back he renewed his complaints of himself to us, with high aggravations of his own cowardice; which gave occasion to some of the Friends tenderly to represent to him the difference between profession and possession, form and power.

He was glad, he said, on our behalfs, that we came off so well, and escaped imprisonment.

But when he understood that George Whitehead and I were liable to an after–reckoning next morning, he was troubled, and wished the morning was come and gone, that we might be gone with it.

We spent the evening in grave conversation and in religious discourses, attributing the deliverance we hitherto had to the Lord. And the next morning, when we were up and had eaten, we tarried some time to see what the Justice would do further with us, and to discharge our engagement to him; the rest of the Friends, who were before fully discharged, tarrying also with us to see the event.

And when we had stayed so long that on all hands it was concluded we might safely go, George Whitehead and I left a few words in writing to be sent to the Justice if he sent after us, importing that we had tarried till such an hour, and not hearing from him, did now hold ourselves free to depart, yet so as that if he should have occasion to send for us again, upon notice thereof we would return.

This done, we took our leave of the family and one of another; they who were for London taking horse, and I and my companions, setting forth on foot for Oxfordshire, went to Wycombe, where we made a short stay to rest and refresh ourselves, and from thence reached our respective homes that night.

After I had spent some time at home, where, as I had no restraint, so (my sisters being gone) I had now no society, I walked up to Chalfont again, and spent a few days with my friends there.

As soon as I came in I was told that my father had been there that day to see Isaac Penington and his wife, but they being abroad at a meeting, he returned to his inn in the town, where he intended to lodge that night. After supper Mary Penington told me she had a mind to go and see him at his inn (the woman of the house being a friend of ours), and I went with her. He seemed somewhat surprised to see me there, because he thought I had been at home at his house; but he took no notice of my hat—at least showed no offence at it, for, as I afterwards understood, he had now an intention to sell his estate, and thought he should need my concurrence therein, which made him now hold it necessary to admit me again into some degree of favour. After we had tarried some little time with him, she rising up to be gone, he waited on her home, and having spent about an hour with us in the family, I waited on him back to his inn. On the way he invited me to come up to London to see my sisters, the younger of whom was then newly married, and directed me where to find them, and also gave me money to defray my charges.

Accordingly I went; yet stayed not long there, but returned to my friend Isaac Penington's, where I made a little stay, and from thence went back to Crowell.

When I was ready to set forth, my friend Isaac Penington was so kind to send a servant with a brace of geldings to carry me as far as I thought fit to ride, and to bring the horses back. I, intending to go no farther that day than to Wycombe, rode no farther than to Beaconsfield town's end, having then but five miles to walk. But here a new exercise befell me, the manner of which was thus:

Before I had walked to the middle of the town I was stopped and taken up by the watch. I asked the watchman what authority he had to stop me, travelling peacefully on the highway: he told me he would show me his authority, and in order thereunto, had me into a house hard by, where dwelt a scrivener whose name was Pepys. To him he gave the order which he had received from the constables, which directed him to take up all rogues, vagabonds, and sturdy beggars. I asked him for which of these he stopped me, but he could not answer me.

I thereupon informed him what a rogue in law is, *viz.*, one who for some notorious offence was burnt on the shoulder; and I told them they might search me if they pleased, and see if I was so branded. A vagabond, I told them, was one that had no dwelling−house nor certain place of abode; but I had, and was going to it, and I told them where it was. And for a beggar, I bade them bring any one that could say I had begged or asked relief.

This stopped the fellow's mouth, yet he would not let me go; but, being both weak−headed and strong−willed, he left me there with the scrivener, and went out to seek the constable, and having found him, brought him thither. He was a young man, by trade a tanner, somewhat better mannered than his wardsman, but not of much better judgment.

He took me with him to his house, and having settled me there, went out to take advice, as I supposed, what to do with me; leaving nobody in the house to guard me but his wife, who had a young child in her arms.

She inquired of me upon what account I was taken up, and seeming to have some pity for me, endeavoured to persuade me not to stay, but to go my way, offering to show me a back way from their house which would bring me into the road again beyond the town, so that none of the town should see me or know what was become of me. But I told her I could not do so.

Then having sat awhile in a muse, she asked me if there was not a place of Scripture which said Peter was at a tanner's house. I told her there was such a Scripture, and directed her where to find it.

After some time she laid her child to sleep in the cradle, and stepped out on a sudden, but came not in again for a pretty while.

I was uneasy that I was left alone in the house, fearing lest if anything should be missing I might be suspected to have taken it; yet I durst not go out to stand in the street, lest it should be thought I intended to slip away.

But besides that, I soon found work to employ myself in; for the child quickly waking, fell to crying, and I was fain to rock the cradle in my own defence, that I might not be annoyed with a noise, to me not more unpleasant than unusual. At length the woman came in again, and finding me nursing the child, gave me many thanks, and seemed well pleased with my company.

When night came on, the constable himself came in again, and told me some of the chief of the town were met together to consider what was fit to do with me, and that I must go with him to them. I went, and he brought me to a little nasty hut, which they called a town–house (adjoining to their market–house), in which dwelt a poor old woman whom they called Mother Grime, where also the watch used by turns to come in and warm themselves in the night.

When I came in among them they looked, some of them, somewhat sourly on me, and asked me some impertinent questions, to which I gave them suitable answers.

Then they consulted one with another how they should dispose of me that night, till they could have me before some justice of peace to be examined. Some proposed that I should be had to some inn, or other public–house, and a guard set on me there. He that started this was probably an innkeeper, and consulted his own interest. Others objected against this, that it would bring a charge on the town, to avoid which they were for having the watch take charge of me, and keep me walking about the streets with them till morning. Most voices seemed to go this way, till a third wished them to consider whether they could answer the doing of that, and the law would bear them out in it: and this put them to a stand. I heard all their debates, but let them alone, and kept my mind to the Lord.

While they thus bandied the matter to and fro, one of the company asked the rest if any of them knew who this young man was, and whither he was going; whereupon the constable to whom I had given both my name and the name of the town where I dwelt, told them my name was Ellwood, and that I lived at a town called Crowell, in Oxfordshire.

Old Mother Grime, sitting by and hearing this, clapped her hand on her knee, and cried out: "I know Mr. Ellwood of Crowell very well; for when I was a maid I lived with his grandfather there when he was a young man." And thereupon she gave them such an account of my father as made them look more regardfully on me; and so Mother Grime's testimony turned the scale, and took me off from walking the rounds with the watch that night.

The constable hereupon bade them take no further care, I should lie at his house that night; and accordingly took me home with him, where I had as good accommodation as the house did afford. Before I went to bed he told me that there was to be a visitation, or Spiritual Court, as he called it, holden next day at Amersham, about four miles from Beaconsfield, and that I was to be carried thither.

This was a new thing to me, and it brought a fresh exercise upon my mind. But being given up in the will of God to suffer what he should permit to be laid on me, I endeavoured to keep my mind quiet and still.

In the morning, as soon as I was up, my spirit was exercised towards the Lord in strong cries to him, that he would stand by me and preserve me, and not suffer me to be taken in the snare of the wicked. While I was thus crying to the Lord the other constable came, and I was called down.

This was a budge fellow, and talked high. He was a shoemaker by trade, and his name was Clark. He threatened me with the Spiritual Court. But when he saw I did not regard it, he stopped, and left the matter to his partner, who pretended more kindness for me, and therefore went about to persuade Clark to let me go out at the back–door, so slip away.

The plot, I suppose, was so laid that Clark should seem averse, but at length yield, which he did, but would have me take it for a favour. But I was so far from taking it so, that I would not take it at all, but told them plainly, that as I came in at the fore–door, so I would go out at the fore–door. When therefore they saw they could not bow me to their will, they brought me out at the fore–door into the street, and wished me a good journey. Yet before I went, calling for the woman of the house, I paid her for my supper and lodging, for I had now got a little money in my pocket again.

After this I got home, as I thought, very well, but I had not been long at home before an illness seized on me, which proved to be the small–pox; of which, so soon as Friends had notice, I had a nurse sent me, and in a while Isaac Penington and his wife's daughter, Gulielma Maria Springett, to whom I had been play–fellow in our infancy, came to visit me, bringing with them our dear friend Edward Burrough, by whose ministry I was called to the knowledge of the truth.

It pleased the Lord to deal favourably with me in this illness, both inwardly and outwardly; for His supporting presence was with me, which kept my spirit near unto Him; and though the distemper was strong upon me, yet I was preserved through it, and my countenance was not much altered by it. But after I was got up again, and while I kept my chamber, wanting some employment for entertainment's sake to spend the time with, and there being at hand a pretty good library of books, amongst which were the works of Augustine and others of those ancient writers who were by many called the fathers, I betook myself to reading. And these books being printed in the old black letter, with abbreviations of the words difficult to be read, I spent too much time therein, and thereby much impaired my sight, which was not strong before, and was now weaker than usual by reason of the illness I had so newly had, which proved an injury to me afterwards, for which reason I here mention it.

After I was well enough to go abroad with respect to my own health and the safety of others, I went up, in the beginning of the twelfth month, 1661, to my friend Isaac Penington's at Chalfont, and abode there some time, for the airing myself more fully, that I might be more fit for conversation.

I mentioned before, that when I was a boy I had made some good progress in learning, and lost it all again before I came to be a man; nor was I rightly sensible of my loss therein until I came amongst the Quakers. But then I both saw my loss and lamented it; and applied myself with utmost diligence, at all leisure times, to recover it; so false I found that charge to be which in those times was cast as a reproach upon the Quakers, that they despised and decried all human learning, because they denied it to be essentially necessary to a gospel ministry, which was one of the controversies of those times.

But though I toiled hard and spared no pains to regain what once I had been master of, yet I found it a matter of so great difficulty that I was ready to say as the noble eunuch to Philip in another case, "How can I, unless I had some man to guide me?"

This I had formerly complained of to my especial friend Isaac Penington, but now more earnestly, which put him upon considering and contriving a means for my assistance.

He had an intimate acquaintance with Dr. Paget, a physician of note in London, and he, with John Milton, a gentleman of great note for learning throughout the learned world, for the accurate pieces he had written on various subjects and occasions.

This person, having filled a public station in the former times, lived now a private and retired life in London, and having wholly lost his sight, kept always a man to read to him, which usually was the son of some gentleman of his acquaintance, whom in kindness he took to improve in his learning.

Thus, by the mediation of my friend Isaac Penington with Dr. Paget, and of Dr. Paget with John Milton, was I admitted to come to him, not as a servant to him (which at that time he needed not), nor to be in the house with him, but only to have the liberty of coming to his house at certain hours when I would, and to read to him what books he should appoint me, which was all the favour I desired.

But this being a matter which would require some time to bring about, I in the meanwhile returned to my father's house in Oxfordshire.

I had before received direction by letters from my eldest sister (written by my father's command) to put off what cattle he had left about his house, and to discharge his servants; which I had done at the time called Michaelmas before. So that all that winter, when I was at home, I lived like a hermit, all alone, having a pretty large house, and nobody in it but myself, at nights especially; but an elderly woman, whose father had been an old servant to the family, came every morning and made my bed, and did what else I had occasion for her to do, till I fell ill of the small-pox, and then I had her with me and the nurse. But now, understanding by letter from my sister that my father did not intend to return to settle there, I made off those provisions which were in the house, that they might not be spoiled when I was gone; and because they were what I should have spent if I had tarried there, I took the money made of them to myself for my support at London, if the project succeeded for my going thither.

This done, I committed the care of the house to a tenant of my father's who lived in the town, and taking my leave of Crowell, went up to my sure friend Isaac Penington again; where understanding that the mediation used for my admittance to John Milton had succeeded so well that I might come when I would, I hastened to London, and in the first place went to wait upon him.

He received me courteously, as well for the sake of Dr. Paget, who introduced me, as of Isaac Penington, who recommended me; to both whom he bore a good respect. And having inquired divers things of me with respect to my former progression in learning, he dismissed me, to provide myself with such accommodation as might be most suitable to my future studies.

I went therefore and took myself a lodging as near to his house (which was then in Jewyn-street) as conveniently as I could, and from thenceforward went every day in the afternoon, except on the first days of the week, and sitting by him in his dining-room read to him in such books in the Latin tongue as he pleased to hear me read.

At my first sitting to read to him, observing that I used the English pronunciation, he told me, if I would have the benefit of the Latin tongue, not only to read and understand Latin authors, but to converse with foreigners, either abroad or at home, I must learn the foreign pronunciation. To this I consenting, he instructed me how to sound the vowels; so different from the common pronunciation used by the English, who speak Anglice their Latin, that—with some few other variations in sounding some consonants in particular cases, as *c* before *e* or *i* like *ch*, *sc* before *i* like *sh*, &c.—the Latin thus spoken seemed as different from that which was delivered, as the English generally speak it, as if it were another language.

I had before, during my retired life at my father's, by unwearied diligence and industry, so far recovered the rules of grammar, in which I had once been very ready, that I could both read a Latin author and after a sort hammer out his meaning. But this change of pronunciation proved a new difficulty to me. It was now harder to me to read than it was before to understand when read. But

Labor omnia vincit
Improbus.

Incessant pains,
The end obtains.

And so did I. Which made my reading the more acceptable to my master. He, on the other hand, perceiving with what earnest desire I pursued learning, gave me not only all the encouragement but all the help he could; for, having a curious ear, he understood by my tone when I understood what I read and when I did not; and accordingly would stop me, examine me, and open the most difficult passages to me.

Thus went I on for about six weeks' time, reading to him in the afternoons; and exercising myself with my own books in my chamber in the forenoons, I was sensible of an improvement.

But, alas! I had fixed my studies in a wrong place. London and I could never agree for health; my lungs, as I suppose, were too tender to bear the sulphurous air of that city, so that I soon began to droop; and in less than two months' time I was fain to leave both my studies and the city, and return into the country to preserve life; and much ado I had to get thither.

I chose to go down to Wycombe, and to John Rance's house there; both as he was a physician, and his wife an honest, hearty, discreet, and grave matron, whom I had a very good esteem of, and who I knew had a good regard for me.

There I lay ill a considerable time, and to that degree of weakness that scarce any who saw me expected my life. But the Lord was both gracious to me in my illness, and was pleased to raise me up again, that I might serve him in my generation.

As soon as I had recovered so much strength as to be fit to travel, I obtained of my father (who was then at his house in Crowell, to dispose of some things he had there, and who in my illness had come to see me) so much money as would clear all charges in the house, for both physic, food, and attendance; and having fully discharged all, I took leave of my friends in that family and in the town, and returned to my studies at London.

I was very kindly received by my master, who had conceived so good an opinion of me that my conversation, I found, was acceptable to him, and he seemed heartily glad of my recovery and return; and into our old method of study we fell again, I reading to him, and he explaining to me, as occasion required.

But as if learning had been a forbidden fruit to me, scarce was I well settled in my work before I met with another diversion, which turned me quite out of my work.

For a sudden storm arising, from I know not what surmise of a plot, and thereby danger to the government, and the meetings of Dissenters— such I mean as could be found, which perhaps were not many besides the Quakers—were broken up throughout the city, and the prisons mostly filled with our friends.

I was that morning, which was the 26th day of the eighth month, 1662, at the meeting at the Bull and Mouth, by Aldersgate, when on a sudden a party of soldiers (of the trained bands of the city) rushed in, with noise and clamour, being led by one who was called Major Rosewell, an apothecary, if I misremember not, and at that time under the ill name of a Papist.

As soon as he was come within the room, having a file or two of musketeers at his heels, he commanded his men to present their muskets at us, which they did, with intent, I suppose, to strike a terror into the people. Then he made a proclamation that all who were not Quakers might depart if they would.

It so happened that a young man, an apprentice in London, whose name was —– Dove, the son of Dr. Dove, of Chinner, near Crowell, in Oxfordshire, came that day in curiosity to see the meeting, and coming early, and finding me there (whom he knew), came and sat down by me.

As soon as he heard the noise of soldiers he was much startled, and asked me softly if I would not shift for myself, and try to get out. I told him no; I was in my place, and was willing to suffer if it was my lot. When he heard the notice given that they who were not Quakers might depart, he solicited me again to be gone. I told him I could not do so, for that would be to renounce my profession, which I would by no means do; but as for him, who was not one of us, he might do as he pleased. Whereupon, wishing me well, he turned away, and with cap in hand went out. And truly I was glad he was gone, for his master was a rigid Presbyterian, who in all likelihood would have led him a wretched life had he been taken and imprisoned among the Quakers.

The soldiers came so early that the meeting was not fully gathered when they came, and when the mixed company were gone out, we were so few, and sat so thin in that large room, that they might take a clear view of us all, and single us out as they pleased.

He that commanded the party gave us first a general charge to come out of the room. But we, who came thither at God's requirings, to worship him, like that good man of old who said, "We ought to obey God rather than men" (Acts v. 29), stirred not, but kept our places. Whereupon he sent some of his soldiers among us, with command to drag or drive us out, which they did roughly enough.

When we came out into the street, we were received there by other soldiers, who with their pikes holden lengthways from one another encompassed us round as sheep in a pound; and there we stood a pretty time, while they were picking up more to add to our number.

In this work none seemed so eager and active as their leader, Major Rosewell; which I observing, stepped boldly to him as he was passing by me, and asked him if he intended a massacre, for of that in those days there was a great apprehension and talk. The suddenness of the question, from such a young man especially, somewhat startled him; but recollecting himself, he answered, "No; but I intend to have you all hanged by the wholesome laws of the land."

When he had gotten as many as he could or thought fit, which were in number thirty–two, whereof two were catched up in the street, who had not been at the meeting, he ordered the pikes to be opened before us; and giving the word to march, went himself at the head of us, the soldiers with their pikes making a lane to keep us from scattering.

He led us up Martin's, and so turned down to Newgate, where I expected he would have lodged us. But, to my disappointment, he went on though Newgate, and turning through the Old Bailey, brought us into Fleet Street. I was then wholly at a loss to conjecture whither he would lead us, unless it were to Whitehall, for I knew nothing then of Old Bridewell; but on a sudden he gave a short turn, and brought us before the gate of that prison, where knocking, the wicket was forthwith opened, and the master, with his porter, ready to receive us.

One of those two who were picked up in the street, being near me, and telling me his case, I stepped to the Major, and told him that this man was not at the meeting, but was taken up in the street; and showed him how hard and unjust a thing it would be to put him into prison.

I had not pleased him before in the question I had put to him about a massacre, and that, I suppose, made this solicitation less acceptable to him from me than it might have been from some other; for looking sternly on me, he said: "Who are you, that take so much upon you? Seeing you are so busy, you shall be the first man that shall go into Bridewell;" and taking me by the shoulders, he thrust me in.

As soon as I was in, the porter, pointing with his finger, directed me to a fair pair of stairs on the farther side of a large court, and bid me go up those stairs and go on till I could go no farther.

Accordingly I went up the stairs; the first flight whereof brought me to a fair chapel on my left hand, which I could look into through the iron grates, but could not have gone into if I would.

I knew that was not a place for me: wherefore, following my direction and the winding of the stairs, I went up a storey higher, which brought me into a room which I soon perceived to be a court–room or place of judicature. After I had stood a while there, and taken a view of it, observing a door on the farther side, I went to it, and opened it, with intention to go in, but I quickly drew back, being almost affrighted at the dismalness of the place; for besides that the walls quite round were laid all over, from top to bottom, in black, there stood in the middle of it a great whipping–post, which was all the furniture it had.

In one of these two rooms judgment was given, and in the other it was executed on those ill people who for their lewdness were sent to this prison, and there sentenced to be whipped; which was so contrived that the court might not only hear, but see, if they pleased, their sentence executed.

A sight so unexpected, and withal so unpleasing, gave me no encouragement either to rest or indeed to enter at all there; till looking earnestly I espied, on the opposite side, a door, which giving me hopes of a farther progress, I adventured to step hastily to it, and opened it.

This let me into one of the fairest rooms that, so far as I remember, I was ever in, and no wonder, for though it was now put to this mean use, it had for many ages past been the royal seat or palace of the kings of England, until Cardinal Wolsey built Whitehall, and offered it as a peace offering to King Henry the Eighth, who until that time had kept his court in this house, and had this, as the people in the house reported, for his dining–room, by which name it then went.

This room in length (for I lived long enough in it to have time to measure it) was threescore feet, and had breadth proportionable to it. In it, on the front side, were very large bay windows, in which stood a large table. It had other very large tables in it, with benches round; and at that time the floor was covered with rushes, against some solemn festival, which I heard it was bespoken for.

Here was my *nil ultra*, and here I found I might set up my pillar; for although there was a door out of it to a back pair of stairs which led to it, yet that was kept locked. So that finding I had now followed my keeper's direction to the utmost point, beyond which I could not go, I sat down and considered that rhetorical saying, "That the way to Heaven lay by the gate of Hell;" the black room, through which I passed into this, bearing some resemblance to the latter, as this comparatively and by way of allusion might in some sort be thought to bear to the former.

But I was quickly put out of these thoughts by the flocking in of the other Friends, my fellow–prisoners, amongst whom yet, when all were come together, there was but one whom I knew so much as by face, and with him I had no acquaintance; for I having been but a little while in the city, and in that time kept close to my studies, I was by that means known to very few.

Soon after we were all gotten together came up the master of the house after us, and demanded our names, which we might reasonably have refused to give till we had been legally convened before some civil magistrate who had power to examine us and demand our names; but we, who were neither guileful nor wilful, simply gave him our names, which he took down in writing.

It was, as I hinted before, a general storm which fell that day, but it lighted most, and most heavily, upon our meetings; so that most of our men Friends were made prisoners, and the prisons generally filled. And great work had the women to run about from prison to prison to find their husbands, their fathers, their brothers, or their servants; for according as they had disposed themselves to several meetings, so were they dispersed to several prisons. And no less care and pains had they, when they had found them, to furnish them with provisions and other necessary accommodations.

But an excellent order, even in those early days, was practised among the Friends of that city, by which there were certain Friends of either sex appointed to have the oversight of the prisons in every quarter, and to take care of all Friends, the poor especially, that should be committed thither.

This prison of Bridewell was under the care of two honest, grave, discreet, and motherly women, whose names were Anne Merrick (afterwards Vivers), and Anne Travers, both widows.

They, so soon as they understood that there were Friends brought into that prison, provided some hot victuals, meat, and broth, for the weather was cold; and ordering their servants to bring it them, with bread, cheese, and beer, came themselves also with it, and having placed it on a table, gave notice to us that it was provided for all those that had not others to provide for them, or were not able to provide for themselves. And there wanted not among us a competent number of such guests.

As for my part, though I had lived as frugally as possibly I could, that I might draw out the thread of my little stock to the utmost length, yet had I by this time reduced it to tenpence, which was all the money I had about me, or anywhere else at my command.

This was but a small estate to enter upon an imprisonment with, yet was I not at all discouraged at it, nor had I a murmuring thought. I had known what it was, moderately, to abound, and if I should now come to suffer want, I knew I ought to be content; and through the grace of God I was so. I had lived by Providence before, when for a long time I had no money at all, and I had always found the Lord a good provider. I made no doubt, therefore, that He who sent the ravens to feed Elijah, and who clothes the lilies, would find some means to sustain me with needful food and raiment; and I had learned by experience the truth of that saying, *Natura paucis contenta—i.e.* Nature is content with few things, or a little.

Although the sight and smell of hot food was sufficiently enticing to my empty stomach, for I had eaten little that morning and was hungry, yet, considering the terms of the invitation, I questioned whether I was included in it; and after some reasonings at length concluded that, while I had tenpence in my pocket, I should be but an injurious intruder to that mess, which was provided for such as perhaps had not twopence in theirs.

Being come to this resolution, I withdrew as far from the table as I could, and sat down in a quiet retirement of mind till the repast was over, which was not long; for there were hands enough at it to make light work of it.

When evening came the porter came up the backstairs, and opening the door, told us if we desired to have anything that was to be had in the house, he would bring it us; for there was in the house a chandler's shop, at which beer, bread, butter, cheese, eggs and bacon, might be had for money. Upon which many went to him, and spake for what of these things they had a mind to, giving him money to pay for them.

Among the rest went I, and intending to spin out my tenpence as far as I could, desired him to bring me a penny loaf only. When he returned we all resorted to him to receive our several provisions, which he delivered; and when he came to me he told me he could not get a penny loaf, but he had brought me two halfpenny loaves.

This suited me better; wherefore returning to my place again, I sat down and eat up one of my loaves, reserving the other for the next day.

This was to me both dinner and supper; and so well satisfied I was with it that I could willingly then have gone to bed, if I had had one to go to; but that was not to be expected there, nor had any one any bedding brought in that night.

Some of the company had been so considerate as to send for a pound of candles, that we might not sit all night in the dark, and having lighted divers of them, and placed them in several parts of that large room, we kept walking to keep us warm.

After I had warmed myself pretty thoroughly and the evening was pretty far spent, I bethought myself of a lodging; and cast mine eye on the table which stood in the bay window, the frame whereof looked, I thought, somewhat like a bedstead. Wherefore, willing to make sure of that, I gathered up a good armful of the rushes wherewith the floor was covered, and spreading them under the table, crept in upon them in my clothes, and keeping on my hat, laid my head upon one end of the table's frame, instead of a bolster.

My example was followed by the rest, who, gathering up rushes as I had done, made themselves beds in other parts of the room, and so to rest we went.

I having a quiet easy mind, was soon asleep, and slept till about the middle of the night. And then waking, finding my legs and feet very cold, I crept out of my cabin and began to walk about apace.

This waked and raised all the rest, who finding themselves cold as well as I, got up and walked about with me, till we had pretty well warmed ourselves, and then we all lay down again, and rested till morning.

Next day, all they who had families, or belonged to families, had bedding brought in of one sort or other, which they disposed at ends and sides of the room, leaving the middle void to walk in.

But I, who had nobody to look after me, kept to my rushy pallet under the table for four nights together, in which time I did not put off my clothes; yet, through the merciful goodness of God unto me, I rested and slept well, and enjoyed health, without taking cold.

In this time divers of our company, through the solicitations of some of their relations or acquaintance to Sir Richard Brown, who was at that time a great master of misrule in the city, and over Bridewell more especially, were released; and among these one William Mucklow, who lay in a hammock. He having observed that I only was unprovided with lodging, came very courteously to me, and kindly offered me the use of his hammock while I should continue a prisoner.

This was a providential accommodation to me, which I received thankfully, both from the Lord and from him; and from thenceforth I thought I lay as well as ever I had done in my life.

Amongst those that remained there were several young men who cast themselves into a club, and laying down every one an equal proportion of money, put it into the hand of our friend Anne Travers, desiring her to lay it out for them in provisions, and send them in every day a mess of hot meat; and they kindly invited me to come into their club with them. These saw my person, and judged of me by that, but they saw not my purse, nor understood the lightness of my pocket. But I, who alone understood my own condition, knew I must sit down with lower commons. Wherefore, not giving them the true reason, I as fairly as I could excused myself from entering at present into their mess, and went on, as before, to eat by myself, and that very sparingly, as my stock would bear; and before my tenpence was quite spent, Providence, on whom I relied, sent me in a fresh supply.

For William Penington, a brother of Isaac Penington's, a Friend and merchant in London, at whose house, before I came to live in the city, I was wont to lodge, having been at his brother's that day upon a visit, escaped this storm, and so was at liberty; and understanding when he came back what had been done, bethought himself of me, and upon inquiry hearing where I was, came in love to see me.

He in discourse, amongst other things, asked me how it was with me as to money, and how well I was furnished: I told him I could not boast of much, and yet I could not say I had none; though what I then had was indeed next to none. Whereupon he put twenty shillings into my hand, and desired me to accept of that for the present. I saw a Divine hand in thus opening his heart and hand in this manner to me; and though I would willingly have been excused from taking so much, and would have returned one half of it, yet he pressing it all upon me, I received it with a thankful acknowledgment as a token of love from the Lord and from him.

On the seventh day he went down again, as he usually did, to his brother's house at Chalfont, and in discourse gave them an account of my imprisonment. Whereupon, at his return on the second day of the week following, my affectionate friend Mary Penington sent me, by him, forty shillings, which he soon after brought me; out of which I would have repaid him the twenty shillings he had so kindly furnished me with, but he would not admit it, telling me I might have occasion for that and more before I got my liberty.

Not many days after this I received twenty shillings from my father, who being then at his house in Oxfordshire, and by letter from my sister understanding that I was a prisoner in Bridewell, sent this money to me for my support there, and withal a letter to my sister for her to deliver to one called Mr. Wray, who lived near Bridewell, and was a servant to Sir Richard Brown in some wharf of his, requesting him to intercede with his master, who was one of the governors of Bridewell, for my deliverance; but that letter coming to my hands, I suppressed it, and have it yet by me.

Now was my pocket from the lowest ebb risen to a full tide. I was at the brink of want, next door to nothing, yet my confidence did not fail nor my faith stagger; and now on a sudden I had plentiful supplies, shower upon shower, so that I abounded, yet was not lifted up, but in humility could say, "This is the Lord's doing." And without defrauding any of the instruments of the acknowledgments due unto them, mine eye looked over and beyond them to the Lord, who I saw was the author thereof and prime agent therein, and with a thankful heart I returned thanksgivings and praises to Him. And this great goodness of the Lord to me I thus record, to the end that all into whose hands this may come may be encouraged to trust in the Lord, whose mercy is over all His works, and who is indeed a God near at hand, to help in the needful time.

Now I durst venture myself into the club to which I had been invited, and accordingly, having by this time gained an acquaintance with them, took an opportunity to cast myself among them; and thenceforward, so long as we continued prisoners there together, I was one of their mess.

And now the chief thing I wanted was employment, which scarce any wanted but myself; for the rest of my company were generally tradesmen of such trades as could set themselves on work. Of these, divers were tailors, some masters, some journeymen, and with these I most inclined to settle. But because I was too much a novice in their art to be trusted with their work, lest I should spoil the garments, I got work from an hosier in Cheapside, which was to make night–waistcoats, of red and yellow flannel, for women and children. And with this I entered myself among the tailors, sitting cross–legged as they did, and so spent those leisure hours with innocency and pleasure which want of business would have made tedious. And indeed that was in a manner the only advantage I had by it; for my master, though a very wealthy man, and one who professed not only friendship but particular kindness to me, dealt I thought but hardly with me. For though he knew not what I had to subsist by, he never offered me a penny for my work till I had done working for him, and went, after I was released, to give him a visit; and then he would not reckon with me neither, because, as he smilingly said, he would not let me so far into his trade as to acquaint me with the prices of the work, but would be sure to give me enough. And thereupon he gave me one crown–piece and no more; though I had wrought long for him, and made him many dozens of waistcoats, and bought the thread myself; which I thought was very poor pay. But as Providence had ordered it, I wanted the work more than the wages, and therefore took what he gave me, without complaining.

About this time, while we were prisoners in our fair chamber, a Friend was brought and put in among us, who had been sent thither by Richard Brown to beat hemp; whose case was thus:

He was a very poor man, who lived by mending shoes, and on a seventh–day night, late, a carman, or some other such labouring man, brought him a pair of shoes to mend, desiring him to mend them that night, that he might have them in the morning, for he had no other to wear. The poor man sat up at work upon them till after midnight, and then finding he could not finish them, went to bed, intending to do the rest in the morning.

Accordingly, he got up betimes, and though he wrought as privately as he could in his chamber, that he might avoid giving offence to any, yet could he not do it so privately but that an ill-natured neighbour perceived it, who went and informed against him for working on the Sunday. Whereupon he was had before Richard Brown, who committed him to Bridewell for a certain time, to be kept to hard labour in beating hemp, which is labour hard enough.

It so fell out that at the same time were committed thither (for what cause I do not now remember) two lusty young men, who were called Baptists, to be kept also at the same labour.

The Friend was a poor little man, of a low condition and mean appearance; whereas these two Baptists were topping blades, that looked high and spoke big. They scorned to beat hemp, and made a pish at the whipping-post; but when they had once felt the smart of it, they soon cried *peccavi*, and submitting to the punishment, set their tender hands to the beetles.

The Friend, on the other hand, acting upon a principle, knowing he had done no evil for which he should undergo that punishment, refused to work, and for refusing was cruelly whipped; which he bore with wonderful constancy and resolution of mind.

The manner of whipping there is, to strip the party to the skin from the waist upwards, and having fastened him to the whipping-post, so that he can neither resist nor shun the strokes, to lash the naked body with long but slender twigs of holly, which will bend almost like thongs, and lap round the body; and these having little knots upon them, tear the skin and flesh, and give extreme pain.

With these rods they tormented the Friend most barbarously and the more for that, having mastered the two braving Baptists, they disdained to be mastered by this poor Quaker. Yet were they fain at last to yield when they saw their utmost severity could not make him yield; and then, not willing to be troubled longer with him, they turned him up among us.

When we had inquired of him how it was with him, and he had given us a brief account of both his cause and usage, it came in my mind that I had in my box (which I had sent for from my lodging, to keep some few books and other necessaries in) a little gallipot with Lucatellu's balsam in it.

Wherefore, causing a good fire to be made, and setting the Friend within a blanket before the fire, we stripped him to the waist, as if he had been to be whipped again, and found his skin so cut and torn with the knotty holly rods, both back, side, arms, and breast, that it was a dismal sight to look upon. Then melting some of the balsam, I with a feather anointed all the sores, and putting a softer cloth between his skin and his shirt, helped him on with his clothes again. This dressing gave him much ease, and I continued it till he was well; and because he was a very poor man, we took him into our mess, contriving that there should always be enough for him as well as for ourselves. Thus he lived with us until the time he was committed for was expired, and then he was released.

But we were still continued prisoners by an arbitrary power, not being committed by the civil authority, nor having seen the face of any civil magistrate from the day we were thrust in here by soldiers, which was the 26th day of the eighth month, to the 19th of the tenth month following.

On that day we were had to the Sessions at the Old Bailey; but not being called there, we were brought back to Bridewell, and continued there to the 29th of the same month, and then we were carried to the Sessions again.

I expected I should have been called the first, because my name was first taken down; but it proved otherwise, so that I was one of the last that was called; which gave me the advantage of hearing the pleas of the other prisoners, and discovering the temper of the Court.

The prisoners complained of the illegality of their imprisonment, and desired to know what they had lain so long in prison for. The Court regarded nothing of that, and did not stick to tell them so, "For," said the Recorder to them, "if you think you have been wrongfully imprisoned, you have your remedy at law, and may take it, if you think it worth your while. The Court," said he, "may send for any man out of the street and tender him the oath: so we take no notice how you came hither, but finding you here, we tender you the oath of allegiance; which if you refuse to take, we shall commit you, and at length præmunire you." Accordingly, as each one refused it, he was set aside and another called.

By this I saw it was in vain for me to insist upon false imprisonment or ask the cause of my commitment; though I had before furnished myself with some authorities and maxims of law on the subject, to have pleaded, if room had been given, and I had the book out of which I took them in my bosom; for the weather being cold, I wore a gown girt about the middle, and had put the book within it. But I now resolved to wave all that, and insist upon another plea, which just then came into my mind.

As soon therefore as I was called I stepped nimbly to the bar, and stood up upon the stepping, that I might the better both hear and be heard, and laying my hands upon the bar, stood ready, expecting what they would say to me.

I suppose they took me for a confident young man, for they looked very earnestly upon me, and we faced each other, without words, for a while. At length the Recorder, who was called Sir John Howel, asked me if I would take the oath of allegiance.

To which I answered: "I conceive this Court hath not power to tender that oath to me, in the condition wherein I stand."

This so unexpected plea seemed to startle them, so that they looked one upon another, and said some what low one to another, "What! doth he demur to the jurisdiction of the Court?" And thereupon the Recorder asked me, "Do you then demur to the jurisdiction of the Court?"—"Not absolutely," answered I, "but conditionally, with respect to my present condition, and the circumstances I am now under."

"Why, what is your present condition?" said the Recorder.—"A prisoner," replied I.—"And what is that," said he, "to your taking or not taking the oath?"—"Enough," said I, "as I conceive, to exempt me from the tender thereof while I am under this condition."—"Pray, what is your reason for that?" said he.—"This," said I, "that if I rightly understand the words of the statute, I am required to say that *I do take this oath freely and without constraint*, which I cannot say, because I am not a free man, but in bonds and under constraint. Wherefore I conceive that if you would tender that oath to me, ye ought first to set me free from my present imprisonment."

"But," said the Recorder, "will you take the oath if you be set free?"—"Thou shalt see that," said I, "when I am set free. Therefore set me free first, and then ask the question."

"But," said he again, "you know your own mind sure, and can tell now what you would do if you were at liberty."—"Yes," replied I, "that I can; but I do not hold myself obliged to tell it until I am at liberty. Therefore set me at liberty, and ye shall soon hear it."

Thus we fenced a good while, till I was both weary of such trifling and doubted also lest some of the standers−by should suspect I would take it if I was set at liberty. Wherefore when the Recorder put it upon me again, I told him plainly, No; though I thought they ought not to tender it me till I had been set at liberty; yet if I was set at liberty I could not take that nor any other oath, because my Lord and Master Christ Jesus had expressly commanded his disciples *not to swear at all.*

As his command was enough to me, so this confession of mine was enough to them. "Take him away, said they; and away I was taken, and thrust into the bail−dock to my other friends, who had been called before me. And as soon as the rest of our company were called, and had refused to swear, we were all committed to Newgate, and thrust into the common side.

When we came there we found that side of the prison very full of Friends, who were prisoners there before (as indeed were at that time all the other parts of that prison, and most of the other prisons about the town), and our addition caused a great throng on that side. Notwithstanding which we were kindly welcomed by our friends whom we found there, and entertained by them as well as their condition would admit, until we could get in our accommodations and provide for ourselves.

We had the liberty of the hall, which is on the first storey over the gate, and which in the daytime is common to all the prisoners on that side, felons as well as others, to walk in and to beg out of; and we had also the liberty of some other rooms over that hall, to walk or work in a−days. But in the night we all lodged in one room, which was large and round, having in the middle of it a great pillar of oaken timber, which bore up the chapel that is over it.

To this pillar we fastened our hammocks at the one end, and to the opposite wall on the other end, quite round the room, and in three degrees, or three storeys high, one over the other; so that they who lay in the upper and middle row of hammocks were obliged to go to bed first, because they were to climb up to the higher by getting into the lower. And under the lower rank of hammocks, by the wall−sides, were laid beds upon the floor, in which the sick and such weak persons as could not get into the hammocks lay. And indeed, though the room was large and pretty airy, yet the breath and steam that came from so many bodies, of different ages, conditions, and constitutions, packed up so close together, was enough to cause sickness amongst us, and I believe did so. For there were many sick and some very weak, though we were not long there, yet in that time one of our fellow-prisoners, who lay in one of those pallet-beds, died.

This caused some bustle in the house; for the body of the deceased being laid out and put into a coffin, was carried down and set in the room called the Lodge, that the coroner might inquire into the cause and manner of his death. And the manner of their doing it is thus: As soon as the coroner is come the turnkeys run out into the street under the gate, and seize upon every man that passes by, till they have got enough to make up the coroner's inquest. And so resolute these rude fellows are, that if any man resist or dispute it with them, they drag him in by main force, not regarding what condition he is of. Nay, I have been told they will not stick to stop a coach, and pluck the men out of it.

It so happened that at this time they lighted on an ancient man, a grave citizen, who was trudging through the gate in great haste, and him they laid hold on, telling him he must come in and serve upon the coroner's inquest. He pleaded hard, begged and besought them to let him go, assuring them he was going on very urgent business, and that the stopping him would be greatly to his prejudice. But they were deaf to all entreaties, and hurried him in, the poor man chafing without remedy.

When they had got their complement, and were shut in together, the rest of them said to this ancient man, "Come, father, you are the oldest among us; you shall be our foreman." And when the coroner had sworn them on the jury, the coffin was uncovered, that they might look upon the body. But the old man, disturbed in his mind at the interruption they had given him, and grown somewhat fretful upon it, said to them: "To what purpose do you show us a dead body here? You would not have us think, sure, that this man died in this room! How then shall we be able to judge how this man came by his death unless we see the place wherein he died, and wherein he hath been kept prisoner before he died? How know we but that the incommodiousness of the place wherein he was kept may have occasioned his death? Therefore show us," said he, "the place wherein this man died."

This much displeased the keepers, and they began to banter the old man, thinking to have beaten him off it. But he stood up tightly to them: "Come come," said he, "though you

91

have made a fool of me in bringing me in hither, ye shall not find a child of me now I am here. Mistake not yourselves: I understand my place and your duty; and I require you to conduct me and my brethren to the place where this man died: refuse it at your peril."

They now wished they had let the old man go about his business, rather than by troubling him have brought this trouble on themselves. But when they saw he persisted in his resolution and was peremptory, the coroner told them they must go show him the place.

It was in the evening when they began this work, and by this time it was grown bedtime with us, so that we had taken down our hammocks, which in the day were hung up by the walls, and had made them ready to go into, and were undressing ourselves in readiness to go into them; when on a sudden we heard a great noise of tongues and of trampling of feet coming up towards us. And by and by one of the turnkeys, opening our door, said: "Hold, hold; do not undress yourselves: here is the coroner's inquest coming to see you."

As soon as they were come to the door, for within the door there was scarce room for them to come, the foreman, who led them, lifting up his hand, said: "Lord bless me! what a sight is here! I did not think there had been so much cruelty in the hearts of Englishmen to use Englishmen in this manner. We need not now question," said he to the rest of the jury, "how this man came by his death; we may rather wonder that they are not all dead, for this place is enough to breed an infection among them. Well," added he, "if it please God to lengthen my life till to-morrow, I will find means to let the King know how his subjects are dealt with."

Whether he did so or not I cannot tell; but I am apt to think that he applied himself to the Mayor or the Sheriffs of London; for the next day one of the Sheriffs, called Sir William Turner, a woollen-draper in Paul's Yard, came to the press-yard, and having ordered the porter of Bridewell to attend him there, sent up a turnkey amongst us, to bid all the Bridewell prisoners come down to him, for they knew us not, but we knew our own company.

Being come before him in the press-yard, he looked kindly on us and spoke courteously to us. "Gentlemen," said he, "I understand the prison is very full, and I am sorry for it. I wish it were in my power to release you and the rest of your friends that are in it. But since I cannot do that, I am willing to do what I can for you, and therefore I am come hither to inquire how it is; and I would have all you who came from Bridewell return thither again, which will be a better accommodation to you, and your removal will give the more room to those that are left behind; and here is the porter of Bridewell, your old keeper, to attend you thither."

We duly acknowledged the favour of the Sheriff to us and our friends above, in this removal of us, which would give them more room and us a better air. But before we parted from him I spoke particularly to him on another occasion, which was this:

When we came into Newgate we found a shabby fellow there among the Friends, who upon inquiry we understood had thrust himself among our friends when they were taken at a meeting, on purpose to be sent to prison with them, in hopes to be maintained by them. They knew nothing of him till they found him shut in with them in the prison, and then took no notice of him, as not knowing how or why he came thither. But he soon gave them cause to take notice of him, for wherever he saw any victuals brought forth for them to eat he would be sure to thrust in, with knife in hand, and make himself his own carver; and so impudent was he, that if he saw the provision was short, whoever wanted, he would be sure to take enough.

Thus lived this lazy drone upon the labours of the industrious bees, to his high content and their no small trouble, to whom his company was as offensive as his ravening was oppressive; nor could they get any relief by their complaining of him to the keepers.

This fellow hearing the notice which was given for the Bridewell men to go down in order to be removed to Bridewell again, and hoping, no doubt, that fresh quarters would produce fresh commons, and that he would fare better with us than where he was, thrust himself amongst us, and went down into the press–yard with us, which I knew not of till I saw him standing there with his hat on, and looking as demurely as he could, that the Sheriff might take him for a Quaker; at the sight of which my spirit was much stirred.

Wherefore, so soon as the Sheriff had done speaking to us and we had made our acknowledgment of his kindness, I stepped a little nearer to him, and pointing to that fellow, said: "That man is not only none of our company, for he is no Quaker, but is an idle, dissolute fellow who hath thrust himself in among our friends to be sent to prison with them, that he might live upon them; therefore I desire we may not be troubled with him at Bridewell."

At this the Sheriff smiled, and calling the fellow forth, said to him: "How came you to be in prison?"—"I was taken at a meeting," said he.—"But what business had you there?" said the Sheriff.—"I went to hear," said he.—"Aye, you went upon a worse design, it seems," replied the Sheriff; "but I'll disappoint you," said he, "for I'll change your company and send you to them that are like yourself." Then calling for the turnkey, he said: "Take this fellow, and put him among the felons, and be sure let him not trouble the Quakers any more."

Hitherto this fellow had stood with his hat on, as willing to have passed, if he could, for a Quaker, but as soon as he heard this doom passed on him, off went his hat, and to bowing and scraping he fell, with "Good your worship, have pity upon me, and set me at liberty."— "No, no," said the Sheriff: "I will not so far disappoint you; since you had a mind to be in prison, in prison you shall be for me." Then bidding the turnkey take him away, he had him up, and put him among the felons, and so Friends had a good deliverance from him.

The Sheriff then bidding us farewell, the porter of Bridewell came to us, and told us we knew our way to Bridewell without him, and he could trust us; therefore he would not stay nor go with us, but left us to take our own time, so we were in before bedtime.

Then went we up again to our friends in Newgate, and gave them an account of what had passed, and having taken a solemn leave of them, we made up our packs to be gone. But before I pass from Newgate, I think it not amiss to give the reader some little account of what I observed while I was there.

The common side of Newgate is generally accounted, as it really is, the worst part of that prison; not so much from the place as the people, it being usually stocked with the veriest rogues and meanest sort of felons and pickpockets, who not being able to pay chamber−rent on the master's side, are thrust in there. And if they come in bad, to be sure they do no go out better; for here they have the opportunity to instruct one another in their art, and impart to each other what improvements they have made therein.

The common hall, which is the first room over the gate, is a good place to walk in when the prisoners are out of it, saving the danger of catching some cattle which they may have left in it, and there I used to walk in a morning before they were let up, and sometimes in the daytime when they have been there.

They all carried themselves respectfully towards me, which I imputed chiefly to this, that when any of our women friends came there to visit the prisoners, if they had not relations of their own there to take care of them, I, as being a young man and more at leisure than most others, for I could not play the tailor there, was forward to go down with them to the grate, and see them safe out. And sometimes they have left money in my hands for the felons, who at such times were very importunate beggars, which I forthwith distributed among them in bread, which was to be had in the place. But so troublesome an office it was, that I thought one had as good have had a pack of hungry hounds about one, as these, when they knew there was a dole to be given. Yet this, I think, made them a little the more observant to me; for they would dispose themselves to one side of the room, that they might make way for me to walk on the other.

For having, as I hinted before, made up our packs and taken our leave of our friends, whom we were to leave behind, we took our bundles on our shoulders, and walked two and two abreast through the Old Bailey into Fleet Street, and so to Old Bridewell. And it being about the middle of the afternoon, and the streets pretty full of people, both the shopkeepers at their doors and passengers in the way would stop us, and ask us what we were and whither we were going; and when we had told them we were prisoners going from one prison to another, from Newgate to Bridewell, "What!" said they, "without a keeper?"—"No," said we, "for our word, which we have given, is our keeper." Some thereupon would advise us not to go to prison, but to go home. But we told them we could not do so; we could suffer for our testimony, but could not fly from it. I do not remember we had any abuse offered us, but were generally pitied by the people.

When we were come to Bridewell, we were not put up into the great room in which we had been before, but into a low room in another fair court, which had a pump in the middle of it. And here we were not shut up as before, but had the liberty of the court to walk in, and of the pump to wash or drink at. And indeed we might easily have gone quite away if we would, there being a passage through the court into the street; but we were true and steady prisoners, and looked upon this liberty, arising from their confidence in us, to be a kind of parole upon us; so that both conscience and honour stood now engaged for our true imprisonment.

Adjoining to this room wherein we were was such another, both newly fitted up for workhouses, and accordingly furnished with very great blocks for beating hemp upon, and a lusty whipping–post there was in each. And it was said that Richard Brown had ordered those blocks to be provided for the Quakers to work on, resolving to try his strength with us in that case; but if that was his purpose, it was overruled, for we never had any work offered us, nor were we treated after the manner of those that are to be so used. Yet we set ourselves to work on them; for being very large, they served the tailors for shop–boards, and others wrought upon them as they had occasion; and they served us very well for tables to eat on.

We had also, besides this room, the use of our former chamber above, to go into when we thought fit; and thither sometimes I withdrew, when I found a desire for retirement and privacy, or had something on my mind to write, which could not so well be done in company. And indeed about this time my spirit was more than ordinarily exercised, though on very different subjects. For, on the one hand, the sense of the exceeding love and goodness of the Lord to me, in His gracious and tender dealings with me, did deeply affect my heart, and caused me to break forth in a song of thanksgiving and praise to Him; and, on the other hand, a sense of the profaneness, debaucheries, cruelties, and other horrid impieties of the age, fell heavy on me, and lay as a pressing weight upon my spirit; and I breathed forth the following hymn to God, in acknowledgment of His great goodness to me, profession of my grateful love to Him, and supplication to Him for the continuance of His kindness to me, in preserving me from the snares of the enemy, and keeping me faithful unto Himself:–

Thee, Thee alone, O God, I fear,
  In Thee do I confide;
Thy presence is to me more dear
  Than all things else beside.
Thy virtue, power, life, and light,
  Which in my heart do shine,
Above all things are my delight:
  O make them always mine!
Thy matchless love constrains my life,
  Thy life constrains my love,
To be to Thee as chaste a wife
  As is the turtle–dove
To her elect, espoused mate,

Whom she will not forsake,
Nor can be brought to violate
  The bond she once did make;
Just so my soul doth cleave to Thee,
  As to her only head,
With whom she longs conjoin'd to be
  In bond of marriage–bed.
But, ah, alas! her little fort
  Is compassed about;
Her foes about her thick resort,
  Within and eke without.
How numerous are they now grown!
  How wicked their intent!
O let thy mighty power be shown,
  Their mischief to prevent.
They make assaults on every side,
  But Thou stand'st in the gap;
Their batt'ring–rams make breaches wide,
  But still Thou mak'st them up.
Sometimes they use alluring wiles
  To draw into their power;
And sometimes weep like crocodiles;
  But all is to devour.
Thus they beset my feeble heart
  With fraud, deceit, and guile,
Alluring her from Thee to start,
  And Thy pure rest defile.
But, oh! the breathing and the moan,
  The sighings of the seed,
The groanings of the grieved one,
  Do sorrows in me breed.
And that immortal, holy birth,
  The offspring of Thy breath
(To whom Thy love brings life and mirth,
  As doth thy absence, death);
That babe, that seed, that panting child,

Which cannot Thee forsake,
In fear to be again beguiled,
  Doth supplication make:
O suffer not Thy chosen one,
  Who puts her trust in Thee,
And hath made Thee her choice alone,
  Ensnared again to be.

Bridewell, London, 1662.

In this sort did I spend some leisure hours during my confinement in Bridewell, especially after our return from Newgate thither, when we had more liberty, and more opportunity and room for retirement and thought: for, as the poet said,

Carmina scribentes secessum et otia quærunt.

  They who would write in measure,
Retire where they may, stillness have and pleasure.

And this privilege we enjoyed by the indulgence of our keeper, whose heart God disposed to favour us. So that both the master and his porter were very civil and kind to us, and had been so indeed all along. For when we were shut up before, the porter would readily let some of us go home in an evening, and stay at home till next morning; which was a great conveniency to men of trade and business, which I being free from, forbore asking for myself, that I might not hinder others.

This he observed, and asked me when I meant to ask to go out; I told him I had not much occasion nor desire, yet at some time or other, perhaps, I might have; but when I had I would ask him but once, and if he then denied me, I would ask him no more.

After we were come back from Newgate I had a desire to go thither again, to visit my friends who were prisoners there, more especially my dear friend and father in Christ, Edward Burrough, who was then a prisoner, with many Friends more, in that part of Newgate which was then called Justice Hall. Whereupon, the porter coming in my way, I asked him to let me go out for an hour or two, to see some friends of mine that evening.

He, to enhance the kindness, made it a matter of some difficulty, and would have me stay till another night. I told him I would be at a word with him, for, as I had told him before that if he denied me I would ask him no more, so he should find I would keep to it.

He was no sooner gone out of my sight but I espied his master crossing the court; wherefore, stepping to him, I asked him if he was willing to let me go out for a little while, to see some friends of mine that evening. "Yes," said he, "very willingly;" and thereupon away walked I to Newgate, where having spent the evening among Friends, I returned in good time.

Under this easy restraint we lay until the Court sat at the Old Bailey again; and then, whether it was that the heat of the storm was somewhat abated, or by what other means Providence wrought it, I know not, we were called to the bar, and, without further question, discharged.

Whereupon we returned to Bridewell again, and having raised some money among us, and therewith gratified both the master and his porter for their kindness to us, we spent some time in a solemn meeting, to return our thankful acknowledgment to the Lord, both for his preservation of us in prison and deliverance of us out of it; and then taking a solemn farewell of each other, we departed with bag and baggage. And I took care to return my hammock to the owner, with due acknowledgment of his great kindness in lending it me.

Being now at liberty, I visited more generally my friends that were still in prison, and more particularly my friend and benefactor William Penington, at his house, and then went to wait upon my Master Milton, with whom yet I could not propose to enter upon my intermitted studies until I had been in Buckinghamshire, to visit my worthy friends Isaac Penington and his virtuous wife, with other friends in that country.

Thither therefore I betook myself, and the weather being frosty, and the ways by that means clean and good, I walked it throughout in a day, and was received by my friends there with such demonstration of hearty kindness as made my journey very easy to me.

I had spent in my imprisonment that twenty shillings which I had received of Wm. Penington, and twenty of the forty which had been sent me from Mary Penington, and had the remainder then about me. That therefore I now returned to her, with due acknowledgment of her husband's and her great care of me, and liberality to me in the time of my need. She would have had me keep it; but I begged of her to accept it from me again, since it was the redundancy of their kindness, and the other part had answered the occasion for which it was sent: and my importunity prevailed.

I intended only a visit hither, not a continuance, and therefore purposed, after I had stayed a few days to return to my lodging and former course in London, but Providence ordered it otherwise.

Isaac Penington had at that time two sons and one daughter, all then very young; of whom the eldest son, John Penington, and the daughter, Mary, the wife of Daniel Wharley, are yet living at the writing of this. And being himself both skilful and curious in pronunciation, he was very desirous to have them well grounded in the rudiments of the English tongue, to which end he had sent for a man out of Lancashire, whom, upon inquiry, he had heard of, who was undoubtedly the most accurate English teacher that ever I met with, or have heard of. His name was Richard Bradley. But as he pretended no higher than the English tongue, and had led them, by grammar rules, to the highest improvement they were capable of in that, he had then taken his leave of them, and was gone up to London, to teach an English school of Friends' children there.

This put my friend to a fresh strait. He had sought for a new teacher to instruct his children in the Latin tongue, as the old had done in the English, but had not yet found one. Wherefore one evening, as we sat together by the fire in his bed–chamber (which for want of health he kept), he asked me, his wife being by, if I would be so kind to him as to stay a while with him till he could hear of such a man as he aimed at, and in the meantime enter his children in the rudiments of the Latin tongue.

This question was not more unexpected than surprising to me, and the more because it seemed directly to thwart my former purpose and undertaking, of endeavouring to improve myself by following my studies with my Master Milton, which this would give at least a present diversion from, and for how long I could not foresee.

But the sense I had of the manifold obligations I lay under to these worthy friends of mine shut out all reasonings, and disposed my mind to an absolute resignation of their desire that I might testify my gratitude by a willingness to do them any friendly service that I could be capable of.

And though I questioned my ability to carry on that work to its due height and proportion, yet as that was not proposed, but an initiation only by accidence into grammar, I consented to the proposal as a present expedient till a more qualified person should be found, without further treaty or mention of terms between us than that of mutual friendship. And to render this digression from my own studies the less uneasy to my mind, I recollected and often thought of that rule in Lilly:

Qui docet indoctos, licet indoctissimus esset,
Ipse brevi reliquis doctior esse queat.

He that the unlearned doth teach may quickly be
More learned than they, though most unlearned he.

With this consideration I undertook this province, and left it not until I married, which was not till the year 1669, near seven years from the time I came thither. In which time, having the use of my friend's books, as well as of my own, I spent my leisure hours much in reading, not without some improvement to myself in my private studies, which (with the good success of my labours bestowed on the children, and the agreeableness of conversation which I found in the family) rendered my undertaking more satisfactory, and my stay there more easy to me.

But, alas! not many days (not to say weeks) had I been there, ere we were almost overwhelmed with sorrow for the unexpected loss of Edward Burrough, who was justly very dear to us all.

This not only good, but great good man, by a long and close confinement in Newgate through the cruel malice and malicious cruelty of Richard Brown, was taken away by hasty death, to the unutterable grief of very many, and unspeakable loss to the Church of Christ in general.

The particular obligation I had to him as the immediate instrument of my convincement, and high affection for him resulting therefrom, did so deeply affect my mind that it was some pretty time before my passion could prevail to express itself in words, so true I found those of the tragedian:

Curæ leves loquuntur,
Ingentes stupent.

Light griefs break forth, and easily get vent,
Great ones are through amazement closely pent.

At length, my muse, not bearing to be any longer mute, broke forth in the following

ACROSTIC,

WHICH SHE CALLED A PATHETIC ELEGY ON THE DEATH OF THAT DEAR AND FAITHFUL SERVANT OF GOD,

EDWARD BURROUGH,

Who died the 14th of the Twelfth Month, 1662.

And thus she introduceth it:

How long shall Grief lie smother'd? ah! how long
Shall Sorrow's signet seal my silent tongue?
How long shall sighs me suffocate? and make
My lips to quiver and my heart to ache?
How long shall I with pain suppress my cries,
And seek for holes to wipe my watery eyes?
Why may not I, by sorrow thus oppressed,
Pour forth my grief into another's breast?
If that be true which once was said by one,
That "He mourns truly who doth mourn alone:" {180}
Then may I truly say, my grief is true,
Since it hath yet been known to very few.
Nor is it now mine aim to make it known
To those to whom these verses may be shown;
But to assuage my sorrow–swollen heart,
Which silence caused to taste so deep of smart.
This is my end, that so I may prevent
The vessel's bursting by a timely vent.

   Quis talia fando
Temperet a lacrymis!

Who can forbear, when such things spoke he hears,
His grave to water with a flood of tears?

E cho ye woods, resound ye hollow places,
L et tears and paleness cover all men's faces.
L et groans, like claps of thunder, pierce the air,
W hile I the cause of my just grief declare,
O that mine eyes could, like the streams of Nile
O 'erflow their watery banks; and thou meanwhile
D rink in my trickling tears, oh thirsty ground,
S o might'st thou henceforth fruitfuler be found.

L ament, my soul, lament; thy loss is deep,
A nd all that Sion love sit down and weep,
M ourn, oh ye virgins, and let sorrow be
E ach damsel's dowry, and (alas, for me!)
N e'er let my sobs and sighings have an end
T ill I again embrace my ascended friend;
A nd till I feel the virtue of his life
T o consolate me, and repress my grief:
I nfuse into my heart the oil of gladness
O nce more, and by its strength remove that sadness
N ow pressing down my spirit, and restore

F ully that joy I had in him before;
O f whom a word I fain would stammer forth,
R ather to ease my heart than show his worth:

H is worth, my grief, which words too shallow are
I n demonstration fully to declare,
S ighs, sobs, my best interpreters now are.

E nvy begone; black Momus quit the place;
N e'er more, Zoilus, show thy wrinkled face,
D raw near, ye bleeding hearts, whose sorrows are
E qual with mine; in him ye had like share.
A dd all your losses up, and ye shall see
R emainder will be nought but woe is me.
E ndeared lambs, ye that have the white stone,
D o know full well his name—it is your own.

E ternitized be that right worthy name;
D eath hath but kill'd his body, not his fame,
W hich in its brightness shall for ever dwell,
A nd like a box of ointment sweetly smell.
R ighteousness was his robe; bright majesty
D ecked his brow; his look was heavenly.

The History of Thomas Ellwood Written by

B old was he in his Master's quarrel, and
U ndaunted; faithful to his Lord's command.
R equiting good for ill; directing all
R ight in the way that leads out of the fall.
O pen and free to ev'ry thirsty lamb;
U nspotted, pure, clean, holy, without blame.
G lory, light, splendour, lustre, was his crown,
H appy his change to him: the loss our own.

Unica post cineres virtus veneranda beatos
Efficit.

Virtue alone, which reverence ought to have,
Doth make men happy, e'en beyond the grave.

While I had thus been breathing forth my grief,
In hopes thereby to get me some relief,
I heard, methought, his voice say, "Cease to mourn:
I live; and though the veil of flesh once worn
Be now stript off, dissolved, and laid aside,
My spirit's with thee, and shall so abide."
This satisfied me; down I shrew my quill,
Willing to be resigned to God's pure will.

Having discharged this duty to the memory of my deceased friend, I went on in my new province, instructing my little pupils in the rudiments of the Latin tongue, to the mutual satisfaction of both their parents and myself. As soon as I had gotten a little money in my pocket, which as a premium without compact I received from them, I took the first opportunity to return to my friend William Penington the money which he had so kindly furnished me with in my need, at the time of my imprisonment in Bridewell, with a due acknowledgment of my obligation to him for it. He was not at all forward to receive it, so that I was fain to press it upon him.

While thus I remained in this family various suspicions arose in the minds of some concerning me with respect to Mary Penington's fair daughter Guli; for she having now arrived at a marriageable age, and being in all respects a very desirable woman—whether regard was had to her outward person, which wanted nothing to render her completely comely; or to the endowments of her mind, which were every way extraordinary and highly obliging; or to her outward fortune, which was fair, and which with some hath not the last nor the least place in consideration—she was openly and secretly sought and solicited by many, and some of them almost of every rank and condition, good and bad, rich and poor, friend and foe. To whom, in their respective turns, till he at length came for whom she was reserved, she carried herself with so much evenness of temper, such courteous freedom, guarded with the strictest modesty, that as it gave encouragement or ground of hopes to none, so neither did it administer any matter of offence or just cause of complaint to any.

But such as were thus either engaged for themselves or desirous to make themselves advocates for others, could not, I observed, but look upon me with an eye of jealousy and fear, that I would improve the opportunities I had by frequent and familiar conversation with her, to my own advantage, in working myself into her good opinion and favour, to the ruin of their pretences.

According therefore to the several kinds and degrees of their fears of me, they suggested to her parents their ill surmises against me.

Some stuck not to question the sincerity of my intentions in coming at first among the Quakers, urging with a why may it not be so, that the desire and hopes of obtaining by that means so fair a fortune might be the prime and chief inducement to me to thrust myself amongst that people? But this surmise could find no place with those worthy friends of mine, her father–in–law and her mother, who, besides the clear sense and sound judgment they had in themselves, knew very well upon what terms I came among them, how strait and hard the passage was to me, how contrary to all worldly interest, which lay fair another way, how much I had suffered from my father for it, and how regardless I had been of attempting or seeking anything of that nature in these three or four years that I had been amongst them.

Some others, measuring me by the propensity of their own inclinations, concluded I would steal her, run away with her, and marry her; which they thought I might be the

106

more easily induced to do, from the advantageous opportunities I frequently had of riding and walking abroad with her, by night as well as by day, without any other company than her maid. For so great indeed was the confidence that her mother had in me, that she thought her daughter safe if I was with her, even from the plots and designs that others had upon her; and so honourable were the thoughts she entertained concerning me, as would not suffer her to admit a suspicion that I could be capable of so much baseness as to betray the trust she with so great freedom reposed in me.

I was not ignorant of the various fears which filled the jealous heads of some concerning me, neither was I so stupid nor so divested of all humanity as not to be sensible of the real and innate worth and virtue which adorned that excellent dame, and attracted the eyes and hearts of so many with the greatest importunity to seek and solicit her. But the force of truth and sense of honour suppressed whatever would have risen beyond the bounds of fair and virtuous friendship; for I easily foresaw that if I should have attempted anything in a dishonourable way by force or fraud upon her, I should have thereby brought a wound upon my own soul, a foul scandal upon my religious profession, and an infamous stain upon mine honour; either of which was far more dear unto me than my life. Wherefore, having observed how some others had befooled themselves by misconstruing her common kindness, expressed in an innocent, open, free, and familiar conversation, springing from the abundant affability, courtesy, and sweetness of her natural temper, to be the effect of a singular regard and peculiar affection to them, I resolved to shun the rock on which I had seen so many run and split; and remembering that saying of the poet,

Felix quem faciunt aliena pericula cautum,

   Happy's he
Whom others' dangers wary make to be,

I governed myself in a free yet respectful carriage towards her, that I thereby both preserved a fair reputation with my friends and enjoyed as much of her favour and kindness in a virtuous and firm friendship as was fit for her to show or for me to seek.

Thus leading a quiet and contented life, I had leisure sometimes to write a copy of verses on one occasion or another, as the poetic vein naturally opened, without taking pains to polish them. Such was this which follows, occasioned by the sudden death of some lusty people in their full strength:

EST VITA CADUCA.

As is the fragrant flower in the field,
Which in the spring a pleasant smell doth yield,
And lovely sight, but soon is withered;
So's Man: to–day alive, to–morrow dead.
And as the silver dew–bespangled grass,
Which in the morn bedecks its mother's face,
But ere the scorching summer's passed looks brown,
Or by the scythe is suddenly cut down.
Just such is Man, who vaunts himself to–day,
Decking himself in all his best array;
But in the midst of all his bravery
Death rounds him in the ear, "Friend, thou must die."
Or like a shadow in a sunny day,
Which in a moment vanishes away;
Or like a smile or spark,—such is the span
Of life allowed this microcosm, Man.
Cease then vain man to boast; for this is true,
Thy brightest glory's as the morning dew,
Which disappears when first the rising sun
Displays his beams above the horizon.

As the consideration of the uncertainty of human life drew the foregoing lines from me, so the sense I had of the folly of mankind, in misspending the little time allowed them in evil ways and vain sports, led me more particularly to trace the several courses wherein the generality of men run unprofitably at best, if not to their hurt and ruin, which I introduced with that axiom of the Preacher (Eccles. i. 2):

ALL IS VANITY.

See here the state of man as in a glass,
And how the fashion of this world doth pass.

Some in a tavern spend the longest day,
While others hawk and hunt the time away.
Here one his mistress courts; another dances;
A third incites to lust by wanton glances.
This wastes the day in dressing; the other seeks
To set fresh colours on her with red cheeks,
That, when the sun declines, some dapper spark
May take her to Spring Garden or the park.
Plays some frequent, and balls; others their prime
Consume at dice; some bowl away their time.
With cards some wholly captivated are;
From tables others scarce an hour can spare.
One to soft music mancipates his ear;
At shovel-board another spends the year.
The Pall Mall this accounts the only sport;
That keeps a racket in the tennis-court.
Some strain their very eyes and throats with singing,
While others strip their hands and backs at ringing.
Another sort with greedy eyes are waiting
Either at cock-pit or some great bull-baiting.
This dotes on running-horses; t'other fool
Is never well but in the fencing-school.
Wrestling and football, nine-pins, prison-base,
Among the rural clowns find each a place.
Nay, Joan unwashed will leave her milking-pail
To dance at May-pole, or a Whitsun ale.
Thus wallow most in sensual delight,

As if their day should never have a night,
Till Nature's pale–faced sergeant them surprise,
And as the tree then falls, just so it lies.
   Now look at home, thou who these lines dost read,
See which of all these paths thyself dost tread,
And ere it be too late that path forsake,
Which, followed, will thee miserable make.

After I had thus enumerated some of the many vanities in which the generality of men misspent their time, I sang the following ode in praise of virtue:–

Wealth, beauty, pleasures, honours, all adieu;
I value virtue far, far more than you.
   You're all but toys
   For girls and boys
To play withal, at best deceitful joys.
She lives for ever; ye are transitory,
Her honour is unstained; but your glory
   Is mere deceit—
   A painted bait,
Hung out for such as sit at Folly's gate.
True peace, content, and joy on her attend;
You, on the contrary, your forces bend
   To blear men's eyes
   With fopperies,
Which fools embrace, but wiser men despise.

About this time my father, resolving to sell his estate, and having reserved for his own use such parts of his household goods as he thought fit, not willing to take upon himself the trouble of selling the rest, gave them unto me; whereupon I went down to Crowell, and having before given notice there and thereabouts that I intended a public sale of them, I sold them, and thereby put some money into my pocket. Yet I sold such things only as I judged useful, leaving the pictures and armour, of which there was some store there, unsold.

Not long after this my father sent for me to come to him at London about some business, which, when I came there, I understood was to join with him in the sale of his estate, which the purchaser required for his own satisfaction and safety, I being then the next heir to it in law. And although I might probably have made some advantageous terms for myself by standing off, yet when I was satisfied by counsel that there was no entail upon it or right of reversion to me, but that he might lawfully dispose of it as he pleased, I readily joined with him in the sale without asking or having the least gratuity or compensation, no, not so much as the fee I had given to counsel to secure me from any danger in doing it.

There having been some time before this a very severe law made against the Quakers by name, and more particularly prohibiting our meetings under the sharpest penalties of five pounds for the first offence so called, ten pounds for the second, and banishment for the third, under pain of felony for escaping or returning without license— which law was looked upon to have been procured by the bishops in order to bring us to a conformity to their way of worship—I wrote a few lines in way of dialogue between a Bishop and a Quaker, which I called

CONFORMITY, PRESSED AND REPRESSED.

B. What! You are one of them that do deny
To yield obedience by conformity.
Q. Nay: we desire conformable to be.
B. But unto what? Q. The Image of the Son. {190}
B. What's that to us! We'll have conformity
Unto our form. Q. Then we shall ne'er have done.
For, if your fickle minds should alter, we
Should be to seek a new conformity.
Thus, who to–day conform to Prelacy,

111

To–morrow may conform to Popery.
But take this for an answer, Bishop, we
Cannot conform either to them or thee;
For while to truth your forms are opposite,
Whoe'er conforms thereto doth not aright.
B. We'll make such knaves as you conform, or lie
Confined in prisons till ye rot and die.
Q. Well, gentle Bishop, I may live to see,
For all thy threats, a check to cruelty;
But in the meantime, I, for my defence,
Betake me to my fortress, Patience.

No sooner was this cruel law made but it was put in execution with great severity; the sense whereof working strongly on my spirit, made me cry earnestly to the Lord that he would arise and set up his righteous judgment in the earth for the deliverance of his people from all their enemies, both inward and outward; and in these terms I uttered it:

Awake, awake, O arm of th' Lord, awake,
  Thy sword uptake;
Cast what would Thine forgetful of Thee make
  Into the lake.
Awake, I pray, O mighty Jah, awake
Make all the world before Thy presence quake,
Not only earth, but heaven also shake.
Arise, arise, O Jacob's God, arise,
  And hear the cries
Of ev'ry soul which in distress now lies,
  And to Thee flies.
Arise, I pray, O Israel's hope, arise;
Set free Thy seed, oppressed by enemies.
Why should they over it still tyrannize?
Make speed, make speed, O Israel's help, make speed,

In time of need;
For evil men have wickedly decreed
   Against Thy seed.
Make speed, I pray, O mighty God, make speed;
Let all Thy lambs from savage wolves be freed,
That fearless on Thy mountain they may feed.
Ride on, ride on, Thou Valiant Man of Might,
   And put to flight
Those sons of Belial who do despite
   To the upright:
Ride on, I say, Thou Champion, and smite
Thine and Thy people's enemies, with such might
That none may dare 'gainst Thee or Thine to fight.

Although the storm raised by the Act for banishment fell with the greatest weight and force upon some other parts, as at London, Hertford, &c., yet we were not in Buckinghamshire wholly exempted therefrom, for a part of that shower reached us also.

For a Friend of Amersham, whose name was Edward Perot or Parret, departing this life, and notice being given that his body would be buried there on such a day, which was the first day of the fifth month, 1665, the Friends of the adjacent parts of the country resorted pretty generally to the burial, so that there was a fair appearance of Friends and neighbours, the deceased having been well–beloved by both.

After we had spent some time together in the house, Morgan Watkins, who at that time happened to be at Isaac Penington's, being with us, the body was taken up and borne on Friends' shoulders along the street in order to be carried to the burying–ground, which was at the town's end, being part of an orchard belonging to the deceased, which he in his lifetime had appointed for that service.

It so happened that one Ambrose Benett, a barrister at law and a justice of the peace for that county, riding through the town that morning on his way to Aylesbury, was by some ill–disposed person or other informed that there was a Quaker to be buried there that day, and that most of the Quakers in the country were come thither to the burial.

Upon this he set up his horses and stayed, and when we, not knowing anything of his design against us, went innocently forward to perform our Christian duty for the interment of our friend, he rushed out of his inn upon us with the constables and a rabble of rude fellows whom he had gathered together, and having his drawn sword in his hand, struck one of the foremost of the bearers with it, commanding them to set down the coffin. But the Friend who was so stricken, whose name was Thomas Dell, being more concerned for the safety of the dead body than his own, lest it should fall from his shoulder, and any indecency thereupon follow, held the coffin fast; which the Justice observing, and being enraged that his word (how unjust soever) was not forthwith obeyed, set his hand to the coffin, and with a forcible thrust threw it off from the bearers' shoulders, so that it fell to the ground in the midst of the street, and there we were forced to leave it.

For immediately thereupon, the Justice giving command for the apprehending us, the constables with the rabble fell on us, and drew some and drove others into the inn, giving thereby an opportunity to the rest to walk away.

Of those that were thus taken I was one. And being, with many more, put into a room under a guard, we were kept there till another Justice, called Sir Thomas Clayton, whom Justice Benett had sent for to join with him in committing us, was come, and then being called forth severally before them, they picked out ten of us, and committed us to Aylesbury gaol, for what neither we nor they knew; for we were not convicted of having either done or said anything which the law could take hold of, for they took us up in the open street, the king's highway, not doing any unlawful act, but peaceably carrying and accompanying the corpse of our deceased friend to bury it, which they would not suffer us to do, but caused the body to lie in the open street and in the cartway, so that all the travellers that passed by, whether horsemen, coaches, carts, or waggons, were fain to break out of the way to go by it, that they might not drive over it, until it was almost night. And then having caused a grave to be made in the unconsecrated part (as it is accounted) of that which is called the churchyard, they forcibly took the body from the widow whose right and property it was, and buried it there.

When the Justices had delivered us prisoners to the constable, it being then late in the day, which was the seventh day of the week, he, not willing to go so far as Aylesbury, nine long miles, with us that night, nor to put the town to the charge of keeping us there that night, and the first day and night following, dismissed us upon our parole to come to

114

him again at a set hour on the second day morning; whereupon we all went home to our respective habitations, and coming to him punctually according to promise, were by him, without guard, conducted to the prison.

The gaoler, whose name was Nathaniel Birch, had not long before behaved himself very wickedly, with great rudeness and cruelty, to some of our friends of the lower side of the county, whom he, combining with the Clerk of the Peace, whose name was Henry Wells, had contrived to get into his gaol; and after they were legally discharged in court, detained them in prison, using great violence, and shutting them up close in the common gaol among the felons, because they would not give him his unrighteous demand of fees, which they were the more straitened in from his treacherous dealing with them. And they having through suffering maintained their freedom and obtained their liberty, we were the more concerned to keep what they had so hardly gained, and therefore resolved not to make any contract or terms for either chamber–rent or fees, but to demand a free prison, which we did.

When we came in, the gaoler was ridden out to wait on the judges, who came in that day to begin the assize, and his wife was somewhat at a loss how to deal with us; but being a cunning woman, she treated us with great appearance of courtesy, offering us the choice of all her rooms; and when we asked upon what terms, she still referred us to her husband, telling us she did not doubt but that he would be very reasonable and civil to us. Thus she endeavoured to have drawn us to take possession of some of her chambers at a venture, and trust to her husband's kind usage. But we, who at the cost of our friends had a proof of his kindness, were too wary to be drawn in by the fair words of a woman, and therefore told her we would not settle anywhere till her husband came home, and then would have a free prison, wheresoever he put us.

Accordingly, walking all together into the court of the prison, in which was a well of very good water, and having beforehand sent to a friend in the town, a widow woman, whose name was Sarah Lambarn, to bring us some bread and cheese, we sat down upon the ground round about the well, and when we had eaten, we drank of the water out of the well.

Our great concern was for our friend Isaac Penington, because of the tenderness of his constitution; but he was so lively in his spirit, and so cheerfully given up to suffer, that he rather encouraged us than needed any encouragement from us.

In this posture the gaoler, when he came home, found us, and having before he came to us consulted his wife, and by her understood on what terms we stood, when he came to us he hid his teeth, and putting on a show of kindness, seemed much troubled that we should sit there abroad, especially his old friend Mr. Penington, and thereupon invited us to come in and take what rooms in his house we pleased. We asked upon what terms; letting him know withal that we determined to have a free prison.

He, like the sun and wind in a fable, that strove which of them should take from the traveller his cloak, having like the wind tried rough, boisterous, violent means to our friends before, but in vain, resolved now to imitate the sun, and shine as pleasantly as he could upon us; wherefore he told us we should make the terms ourselves, and be as free as we desired if we thought fit, when we were released, to give him anything, he would thank us for it, and if not, he would demand nothing.

Upon these terms we went in and disposed ourselves, some in the dwelling–house, others in the malt–house, where they chose to be.

During the assize we were brought before Judge Morton, a sour, angry man, who very rudely reviled us, but would not either hear us or the cause, but referred the matter to the two justices who had committed us.

They, when the assize was ended, sent for us to be brought before them at their inn, and fined us, as I remember, six shillings and eightpence apiece, which we not consenting to pay, they committed us to prison again for one month from that time, on the Act for banishment.

When we had lain there that month, I, with another, went to the gaoler to demand our liberty, which he readily granted, telling us the door should be opened when we pleased to go.

This answer of his I reported to the rest of my friends there, and thereupon we raised among us a small sum of money, which they put into my hand for the gaoler, whereupon I, taking another with me, went to the gaoler with the money in my hand, and reminding him of the terms upon which we accepted the use of his rooms, I told him, that although we could not pay chamber rent or fees, yet inasmuch as he had now been civil to us, we were willing to acknowledge it by a small token, and thereupon gave him the money. He, putting it into his pocket, said, "I thank you and your friends for it, and to let you see I take it as a gift, not a debt, I will not look on it to see how much it is."

The prison door being then set open for us, we went out, and departed to our respective homes.

But before I left the prison, considering one day with myself the different kinds of liberty and confinement, freedom and bondage, I took my pen, and wrote the following enigma or riddle:–

Lo! here a riddle to the wise,
In which a mystery there lies;
Read it, therefore, with that eye
Which can discern a mystery.

THE RIDDLE.

Some men are free while they in prison lie;
Others, who ne'er saw prison, captives die.

CAUTION.

He that can receive it may;
He that cannot, let him stay,
And not be hasty, but suspend
His judgment till he sees the end.

SOLUTION.

He only's free indeed that's free from sin,
And he is safest bound that's bound therein.

CONCLUSION.

This is the liberty I chiefly prize,
The other, without this, I can despise.

Some little time before I went to Aylesbury prison I was desired by my quondam master, Milton, to take a house for him in the neighbourhood where I dwelt, that he might go out of the city, for the safety of himself and his family, the pestilence then growing hot in London. I took a pretty box for him in Giles Chalfont, a mile from me, of which I gave him notice, and intended to have waited on him, and seen him well settled in it, but was prevented by that imprisonment.

But now being released and returned home, I soon made a visit to him, to welcome him into the country.

After some common discourses had passed between us, he called for a manuscript of his; which being brought he delivered to me, bidding me take it home with me, and read it at my leisure; and when I had so done, return it to him with my judgment thereupon.

When I came home, and had set myself to read it, I found it was that excellent poem which he entitled "Paradise Lost." After I had, with the best attention, read it through, I made him another visit, and returned him his book, with due acknowledgment of the favour he had done me in communicating it to me. He asked me how I liked it and what I thought of it, which I modestly but freely told him, and after some further discourse about it, I pleasantly said to him, "'Thou hast said much here of Paradise Lost,' but what hast thou to say of 'Paradise Found?'" He made me no answer, but sat some time in a muse; then brake off that discourse, and fell upon another subject.

After the sickness was over, and the city well cleansed and become safely habitable again, he returned thither. And when afterwards I went to wait on him there, which I seldom failed of doing whenever my occasions drew me to London, he showed me his second poem, called "Paradise Regained," and in a pleasant tone said to me, "This is owing to you, for you put it into my head by the question you put to me at Chalfont, which before I had not thought of." But from this digression I return to the family I then lived in.

We had not been long at home, about a month perhaps, before Isaac Penington was taken out of his house in an arbitrary manner by military force, and carried prisoner to Aylesbury gaol again, where he lay three–quarters of a year, with great hazard of his life, it being the sickness year, and the plague being not only in the town, but in the gaol.

Meanwhile his wife and family were turned out of his house, called the Grange, at Peter's Chalfont, by them who had seized upon his estate; and the family being by that means broken up, some went one way, others another. Mary Penington herself, with her younger children, went down to her husband at Aylesbury. Guli, with her maid, went to Bristol, to see her former maid, Anne Hersent, who was married to a merchant of that city, whose name was Thomas Biss; and I went to Aylesbury with the children, but not finding the place agreeable to my health, I soon left it, and returning to Chalfont, took a lodging, and was dieted in the house of a friendly man, and after some time went to Bristol to conduct Guli home.

Meanwhile Mary Penington took lodgings in a farmhouse called Bottrels, in the parish of Giles Chalfont, where, when we returned from Bristol, we found her.

We had been there but a very little time before I was sent to prison again upon this occasion. There was in those times a meeting once a month at the house of George Salter, a Friend, of Hedgerly, to which we sometimes went; and Morgan Watkins being with us, he and I, with Guli and her maid, and one Judith Parker, wife of Dr. Parker, one of the College of Physicians at London, with a maiden daughter of theirs, neither of whom were Quakers, but as acquaintances of Mary Penington were with her on a visit, walked over to that meeting, it being about the middle of the first month, and the weather good.

This place was about a mile from the house of Ambrose Benett, the justice who the summer before had sent me and some other Friends to Aylesbury prison from the burial of Edward Parret of Amersham; and he, by what means I know not, getting notice not only of the meeting, but, as was supposed, of our being there, came himself to it, and as he came caught up a stackwood stick, big enough to have knocked any man down, and brought it with him, hidden under his cloak.

Being come to the house, he stood for a while without the door and out of sight, listening to hear what was said, for Morgan was then speaking in the meeting. But certainly he heard very imperfectly, if it was true which we heard he said afterwards among his companions, as an argument, that Morgan was a Jesuit—viz., that in his preaching he trolled over his Latin as fluently as ever he heard any one; whereas Morgan, good man, was better versed in Welsh than in Latin, which I suppose he had never learned: I am sure he did not understand it.

When this martial Justice, who at Amersham had with his drawn sword struck an unarmed man who he knew would not strike again, had now stood some time abroad, on a sudden he rushed in among us, with the stackwood stick held up in his hand ready to strike, crying out, "Make way there;" and an ancient woman not getting soon enough out of his way, he struck her with the stick a shrewd blow over the breast. Then pressing through the crowd to the place where Morgan stood, he plucked him from thence, and caused so great a disorder in the room that it broke the meeting up; yet would not the people go away or disperse themselves, but tarried to see what the issue would be.

Then taking pen and paper, he sat down at the table among us, and asked several of us our names, which we gave, and he set down in writing.

Amongst others he asked Judith Parker, the doctor's wife, what her name was, which she readily gave; and thence taking occasion to discourse him, she so overmastered him by clear reason, delivered in fine language, that he, glad to be rid of her, struck out her name and dismissed her; yet did not she remove, but kept her place amongst us.

When he had taken what number of names he thought fit, he singled out half a dozen, whereof Morgan was one, I another, one man more, and three women, of whom the woman of the house was one, although her husband then was, and for divers years before had been, a prisoner in the Fleet for tithes, and had nobody to take care of his family and business but her his wife.

Us six he committed to Aylesbury gaol, which when the doctor's wife heard him read to the constable, she attacked him again, and having put him in mind that it was a sickly time, and that the pestilence was reported to be in that place, she in handsome terms desired him to consider in time how he would answer the cry of our blood, if by his sending us to be shut up in an infected place we should lose our lives there. This made him alter his purpose, and by a new mittimus sent us to the House of Correction at Wycombe. And although he committed us upon the Act for banishment, which limited a certain time for imprisonment, yet he in his mittimus limited no time, but ordered us to be kept till we should be delivered by due course of law; so little regardful was he, though a lawyer, of keeping to the letter of the law.

We were committed on the 13th day of the month called March, 1665, and were kept close prisoners there till the 7th day of the month called June, which was some days above twelve weeks, and much above what the Act required.

Then were we sent for to the Justice's house, and the rest being released, Morgan Watkins and I were required to find sureties for our appearance at the next assize; which we refusing to do, were committed anew to our old prison, the House of Correction at Wycombe, there to lie until the next assizes; Morgan being in this second mittimus represented as a notorious offender in preaching, and I as being upon the second conviction in order to banishment. There we lay till the 25th day of the same month, and then, by the favour of the Earl of Ancram, being brought before him at his house, we were discharged from the prison upon our promise to appear, if at liberty and in health, at the assizes; which we did, and were there discharged by proclamation.

During my imprisonment in this prison I betook myself for an employment to making of nets for kitchen−service, to boil herbs, &c., in which trade I learned of Morgan Watkins, and selling some and giving others, I pretty well stocked the Friends of that country with them.

Though in that confinement I was not very well suited with company for conversation, Morgan's natural temper not being very agreeable to mine, yet we kept a fair and brotherly correspondence, as became friends, prison−fellows, and bed−fellows, which we were. And indeed it was a good time, I think, to us all, for I found it so to me; the Lord being graciously pleased to visit my soul with the refreshing dews of his divine life, whereby my spirit was more and more quickened to Him, and truth gained ground in me over the temptations and snares of the enemy; which frequently raised in my heart thanksgivings and praises unto the Lord. And at one time more especially the sense I had of the prosperity of truth, and the spreading thereof, filling my heart with abundant joy, made my cup overflow, and the following lines drop out:−

For truth I suffer bonds, in truth I live,
   And unto truth this testimony give,
That truth shall over all exalted be,
   And in dominion reign for evermore:
The child's already born that this may see,
   Honour, praise, glory be to God therefor.

And underneath thus:

Though death and hell should against truth combine,
Its glory shall through all their darkness shine.

This I saw with an eye of faith, beyond the reach of human sense; for,

   As strong desire
   Draws objects nigher
In apprehension than indeed they are;
   I with an eye
   That pierced high
Did thus of truth's prosperity declare.

After we had been discharged at the assizes I returned to Isaac Penington's family at Bottrel's in Chalfont, and, as I remember, Morgan Watkins with me, leaving Isaac Penington a prisoner in Aylesbury goal.

The lodgings we had in this farmhouse (Bottrel's) proving too strait and inconvenient for the family, I took larger and better lodgings for them in Berriehouse at Amersham, whither we went at the time called Michaelmas, having spent the summer at the other place.

Some time after was that memorable meeting appointed to be held at London, through a divine opening in the motion of life, in that eminent servant and prophet of God, George Fox, for the restoring and bringing in again those who had gone out from truth, and the holy unity of Friends therein, by the means and ministry of John Perrot.

This man came pretty early amongst Friends, and too early took upon him the ministerial office; and being, though little in person, yet great in opinion of himself, nothing less would serve him than to go and convert the Pope; in order whereunto, he having a better man than himself, John Luff, to accompany him, travelled to Rome, where they had not been long ere they were taken up and clapped into prison. Luff, as I remember, was put in the Inquisition, and Perrot in their Bedlam, or hospital for madmen.

Luff died in prison, not without well–grounded suspicion of being murdered there; but Perrot lay there some time, and now and then sent over an epistle to be printed here, written in such an affected and fantastic style as might have induced an indifferent reader to believe they had suited the place of his confinement to his condition.

After some time, through the mediation of Friends (who hoped better of him than he proved) with some person of note and interest there, he was released, and came back for England. And the report of his great sufferings there (far greater in report than in reality), joined with a singular show of sanctity, so far opened the hearts of many tender and compassionate Friends towards him, that it gave him the advantage of insinuating himself into their affections and esteem, and made way for the more ready propagation of that peculiar error of his, of keeping on the hat in time of prayer as well public as private, unless they had an immediate motion at that time to put it off.

Now, although I had not the least acquaintance with this man, not having ever exchanged a word with him, though I knew him by sight, nor had I any esteem for him, for either his natural parts or ministerial gift, but rather a dislike of his aspect, preaching, and way of writing; yet this error of his being broached in the time of my infancy and weakness of judgment as to truth, while I lived privately in London and had little converse with

Friends, I, amongst the many who were caught in that snare, was taken with the notion, as what then seemed to my weak understanding suitable to the doctrine of a spiritual dispensation. And the matter coming to warm debates, both in words and writing, I, in a misguided zeal, was ready to have entered the lists of contention about it, not then seeing what spirit it proceeded from and was managed by, nor foreseeing the disorder and confusion in worship which must naturally attend it.

But as I had no evil intention or sinister end in engaging in it, but was simply betrayed by the specious pretence and show of greater spirituality, the Lord, in tender compassion to my soul, was graciously pleased to open my understanding and give me a clear sight of the enemy's design in this work, and drew me off from the practice of it, and to bear testimony against it as occasion offered.

But when that solemn meeting was appointed at London for a travail in spirit on behalf of those who had thus gone out, that they might rightly return and be sensibly received into the unity of the body again, my spirit rejoiced, and with gladness of heart I went to it, as did many more of both city and country, and with great simplicity and humility of mind did honestly and openly acknowledge our outgoing, and take condemnation and shame to ourselves. And some that lived at too remote a distance in this nation as well as beyond the seas, upon notice given of that meeting and the intended service of it, did the like by writing in letters directed to and openly read in the meeting, which for that purpose was continued many days.

Thus in the motion of life were the healing waters stirred and many through the virtuous power thereof restored to soundness, and indeed not many lost. And though most of those who thus returned were such as with myself had before renounced the error and forsaken the practice, yet did we sensibly find that forsaking without confessing, in case of public scandal, was not sufficient, but that an open acknowledgment of open offences as well as forsaking them, was necessary to the obtaining complete remission.

Not long after this, George Fox was moved of the Lord to travel through the countries, from county to county, to advise and encourage Friends to set up monthly and quarterly meetings, for the better ordering the affairs of the church in taking care of the poor, and exercising a true gospel discipline for a due dealing with any that might walk disorderly under our name, and to see that such as should marry among us did act fairly and clearly in that respect.

When he came into this county I was one of the many Friends that were with him at the meeting for that purpose; and afterwards I travelled with Guli and her maid into the West of England to meet him there and to visit Friends in those parts, and we went as far as Topsham in Devonshire before we found him. He had been in Cornwall, and was then returning, and came in unexpectedly at Topsham, where we then were providing (if he had not then come thither) to have gone that day towards Cornwall. But after he was come to us we turned back with him through Devonshire, Somersetshire, and Dorsetshire, having generally very good meetings where he was; and the work he was chiefly concerned in went on very prosperously and well, without any opposition or dislike, save in that in the general meeting of Friends in Dorsetshire a quarrelsome man, who had gone out from Friends in John Perrot's business and had not come rightly in again, but continued in the practice of keeping on his hat in time of prayer, to the great trouble and offence of Friends, began to cavil and raise disputes, which occasioned some interruption and disturbance.

Not only George and Alexander Parker, who were with him, but divers of the ancient Friends of that country, endeavoured to quiet that troublesome man and make him sensible of his error, but his unruly spirit would still be opposing what was said unto him and justifying himself in that practice. This brought a great weight and exercise upon me, who sat at a distance in the outward part of the meeting, and after I had for some time bore the burden thereof, I stood up in the constraining power of the Lord, and in great tenderness of spirit declared unto the meeting, and to that person more particularly, how it had been with me in that respect, how I had been betrayed into that wrong practice, how strong I had been therein, and how the Lord had been graciously pleased to show me the evil thereof, and recover me out of it.

This coming unexpectedly from me, a young man, a stranger, and one who had not intermeddled with the business of the meeting, had that effect upon the caviller, that if it did not satisfy him, it did at least silence him, and made him for the present sink down and be still, without giving any further disturbance to the meeting. And the Friends were well pleased with this unlooked-for testimony from me, and I was glad that I had that opportunity to confess to the truth, and to acknowledge once more, in so public a manner, the mercy and goodness of the Lord to me therein.

By the time we came back from this journey the summer was pretty far gone, and the following winter I spent with the children of the family as before, without any remarkable alteration in my circumstances, until the next spring, when I found in myself a disposition of mind to change my single life for a married state.

I had always entertained so high a regard for marriage, as it was a divine institution, that I held it not lawful to make it a sort of political trade, to rise in the world by. And therefore as I could not but in my judgment blame such as I found made it their business to hunt after and endeavour to gain those who were accounted great fortunes, not so much regarding what she is as what she has, but making wealth the chief if not the only thing they aimed at; so I resolved to avoid, in my own practice, that course, and how much soever my condition might have prompted me, as well as others, to seek advantage that way, never to engage on account of riches, nor at all to marry till judicious affection drew me to it, which I now began to feel at work in my breast.

The object of this affection was a Friend whose name was Mary Ellis, whom for divers years I had had an acquaintance with, in the way of common friendship only, and in whom I thought I then saw those fair prints of truth and solid virtue which I afterwards found in a sublime degree in her; but what her condition in the world was as to estate, I was wholly a stranger to, nor desired to know.

I had once, a year or two before, had an opportunity to do her a small piece of service, which she wanted some assistance in, wherein I acted with all sincerity and freedom of mind, not expecting or desiring any advantage by her, or reward from her, being very well satisfied in the act itself that I had served a Friend and helped the helpless.

That little intercourse of common kindness between us ended without the least thought I am verily persuaded on her part, well assured on my own, of any other or further relation than that of free and fair friendship, nor did it at that time lead us into any closer conversation or more intimate acquaintance one with the other than had been before.

But some time, and that a good while after, I found my heart secretly drawn and inclining towards her, yet was I not hasty in proposing, but waited to feel a satisfactory settlement of mind therein, before I made any step thereto.

After some time I took an opportunity to open my mind therein unto my much-honoured friends Isaac and Mary Penington, who then stood *parentum loco* (in the place or stead of parents) to me. They having solemnly weighed the matter, expressed their unity therewith; and indeed their approbation thereof was no small confirmation to me therein. Yet took I further deliberation, often retiring in spirit to the Lord, and crying to Him for direction, before I addressed myself to her. At length, as I was sitting all alone, waiting upon the Lord for counsel and guidance in this—in itself and to me—so important affair, I felt a word sweetly arise in me, as if I had heard a voice which said, "Go, and prevail." And faith springing in my heart with the word, I immediately arose and went, nothing doubting.

When I was come to her lodgings, which were about a mile from me, her maid told me she was in her chamber, for having been under some indisposition of body, which had obliged her to keep her chamber, she had not yet left it; wherefore I desired the maid to acquaint her mistress that I was come to give her a visit, whereupon I was invited to go up to her. And after some little time spent in common conversation, feeling my spirit weightily concerned, I solemnly opened my mind unto her with respect to the particular business I came about, which I soon perceived was a great surprise to her, for she had taken in an apprehension, as others also had done, that mine eye had been fixed elsewhere and nearer home.

I used not many words to her, but I felt a divine power went along with the words, and fixed the matter expressed by them so fast in her breast, that, as she afterwards acknowledged to me, she could not shut it out.

I made at that time but a short visit, for having told her I did not expect an answer from her now, but desired she would in the most solemn manner weigh the proposal made, and in due time give me such an answer thereunto as the Lord should give her, I took my leave of her and departed, leaving the issue to the Lord.

I had a journey then at hand, which I foresaw would take me up two weeks' time. Wherefore, the day before I was to set out I went to visit her again, to acquaint her with my journey, and excuse my absence, not yet pressing her for an answer, but assuring her that I felt in myself an increase of affection to her, and hoped to receive a suitable return from her in the Lord's time, to whom in the meantime I committed both her, myself, and the concern between us. And indeed I found at my return that I could not have left it in better hands; for the Lord had been my advocate in my absence, and had so far answered all her objections that when I came to her again she rather acquainted me with them than urged them.

From that time forward we entertained each other with affectionate kindness in order to marriage, which yet we did not hasten to, but went on deliberately. Neither did I use those vulgar ways of courtship, by making frequent and rich presents, not only for that my outward condition would not comport with the expense, but because I liked not to obtain by such means, but preferred an unbribed affection.

While this affair stood thus with me, I had occasion to take another journey into Kent and Sussex, which yet I would not mention here, but for a particular accident which befell me on the way.

The occasion of this journey was this. Mary Penington's daughter Guli, intending to go to her Uncle Springett's, in Sussex, and from thence amongst her tenants, her mother desired me to accompany her, and assist her in her business with her tenants.

We tarried at London the first night, and set out next morning on the Tunbridge road, and Seven Oaks lying in our way we put in there to bait; but truly we had much ado to get either provisions or room for ourselves or our horses, the house was so filled with guests, and those not of the better sort. For the Duke of York being, as we were told, on the road that day for the Wells, divers of his guards and the meaner sort of his retinue had near filled all the inns there.

I left John Gigger, who waited on Guli in this journey and was afterwards her menial servant, to take care of the horses, while I did the like as well as I could for her. I got a little room to put her into, and having shut her into it, went to see what relief the kitchen would afford us, and with much ado, by praying hard and paying dear, I got a small joint of meat from the spit, which served rather to stay than satisfy our stomachs, for we were all pretty sharp set.

After this short repast, being weary of our quarters, we quickly mounted and took the road again, willing to hasten from a place where we found nothing but rudeness; a knot of [rude people] soon followed us, designing, as we afterwards found, to put an abuse upon us, and make themselves sport with us. We had a spot of fine smooth sandy way, whereon the horses trod so softly that we heard them not till one of them was upon us. I was then riding abreast with Guli, and discoursing with her, when on a sudden hearing a little noise, and turning mine eye that way, I saw a horseman coming up on the further side of her horse, having his left arm stretched out, just ready to take her about the waist and pluck her off backwards from her own horse to lay her before him upon his. I had but just time to thrust forth my stick between him and her, and bid him stand off, and at the same time reining my horse to let hers go before me, thrust in between her and him, and being better mounted than he my horse ran him off. But his horse being, though weaker than mine, yet nimble, he slipped by me and got up to her on the near side, endeavouring to offer abuse to her, to prevent which I thrust in upon him again, and in our jostling we drove her horse quite out of the way and almost into the next hedge.

While we were thus contending I heard a noise of loud laughter behind us, and turning my head that way I saw three or four horsemen more, who could scarce sit their horses for laughing to see the sport their companion made with us. From thence I saw it was a plot laid, and that this rude fellow was not to be dallied with; wherefore I bestirred myself the more to keep him off, admonishing him to take warning in time and give over his abusiveness, lest he repented too late. He had in his hand a short thick truncheon, which he held up at me, on which laying hold with a strong grip, I suddenly wrenched it out of his hand, and threw it at as far a distance behind me as I could.

While he rode back to fetch his truncheon, I called up honest John Gigger, who was indeed a right honest man, and of a temper so thoroughly peaceable that he had not hitherto put in at all; but now I roused him, and bade him ride so close up to his mistress's horse on the further side that no horse might thrust in between, and I would endeavour to guard the near side. But he, good man, not thinking it perhaps decent enough for him to ride so near his mistress, left room enough for another to ride between. And indeed so soon as our brute had recovered his truncheon, he came up directly thither, and had thrust in again, had not I, by a nimble turn, chopped in upon him, and kept him at bay.

I then told him I had hitherto spared him, but wished him not to provoke me further. This I spoke with such a tone as bespoke a high resentment of the abuse put upon us, and withal pressed so close upon him with my horse that I suffered him not to come up any more to Guli.

This his companions, who kept an equal distance behind us, both heard and saw, and thereupon two of them advancing, came up to us. I then thought I might likely have my hands full, but Providence turned it otherwise; for they, seeing the contest rise so high, and probably fearing it would rise higher, not knowing where it might stop, came in to part us, which they did by taking him away, one of them leading his horse by the bridle, and the other driving him on with his whip, and so carried him off.

One of their company stayed yet behind; and it so happening that a great shower just then fell, we betook ourselves for shelter to a thick and well–spread oak which stood hard by. Thither also came that other person, who wore the Duke's livery, and while we put on our defensive garments against the weather, which then set in to be wet, he took the opportunity to discourse with me about the man that had been so rude to us, endeavouring to excuse him by alleging that he had drank a little too liberally. I let him know that one vice would not excuse another; that although but one of them was actually concerned in the abuse, yet both he and the rest of them were abettors of it and accessories to it; that I was not ignorant whose livery they wore, and was well assured their lord would not maintain them in committing such outrages upon travellers on the road, to our injury and his dishonour; that I understood the Duke was coming down, and that they might expect to be called to an account for this rude action.

He then begged hard that we would pass by the offence, and make no complaint to their lord; for, he knew, he said, the Duke would be very severe, and it would be the utter ruin of the young man. When he had said what he could, he went off before us, without any ground given him to expect favour; and when we had fitted ourselves for the weather we followed after our own pace.

When we came to Tunbridge I set John Gigger foremost, bidding him lead on briskly through the town, and placing Guli in the middle, I came close up after her that I might both observe and interpose if any fresh abuse should have been offered her. We were expected, I perceived, for though it rained very hard, the street was thronged with men, who looked very earnestly on us, but did not put any affront upon us.

We had a good way to ride beyond Tunbridge and beyond the Wells, in byeways among the woods, and were the later for the hindrance we had had on the way. And when, being come to Harbert Springett's house, Guli acquainted her uncle what danger and trouble she had gone through on the way, he resented it so high that he would have had the persons prosecuted for it; but since Providence had interposed, and so well preserved and delivered her, she chose to pass by the offence.

When Guli had finished the business she went upon, we returned home, and I delivered her safe to her glad mother. From that time forward I continued my visits to my best beloved Friend until we married, which was on the 28th day of the eighth month, called October, in the year 1669. We took each other in a select meeting of the ancient and grave Friends of that country, holden in a Friend's house, where in those times not only the monthly meeting for business but the public meeting for worship was sometimes kept. A very solemn meeting it was, and in a weighty frame of spirit we were, in which we sensibly felt the Lord with us, and joining us; the sense whereof remained with us all our lifetime, and was of good service and very comfortable to us on all occasions.

My next care after marriage was to secure my wife what moneys she had, and with herself bestowed upon me; for I held it would be an abominable crime in me, and savour of the highest ingratitude, if I, though but through negligence, should leave room for my father, in case I should be taken away suddenly, to break in upon her estate, and deprive her of any part of that which had been and ought to be her own. Wherefore with the first opportunity—as I remember, the very next day, and before I knew particularly what she had—I made my will, and thereby secured to her whatever I was possessed of as well all that which she brought, either in moneys or in goods, as that little which I had before I married her; which indeed was but little, yet more by all that little than I had ever given her ground to expect with me.

She had indeed been advised by some of her relations to secure before marriage some part at least of what she had, to be at her own disposal; which, though perhaps not wholly free from some tincture of self−interest in the proposer, was not in itself the worst of counsel. But the worthiness of her mind, and the sense of the ground on which she received me, would not suffer her to entertain any suspicion of me; and this laid on me the greater obligation, in point of gratitude as well as of justice, to regard and secure her; which I did.

I had not been long married before I was solicited by my dear friends Isaac and Mary Penington, and her daughter Guli, to take a journey into Kent and Sussex to account with their tenants and overlook their estates in those counties, which before I was married I had had the care of; and accordingly the journey I undertook, though in the depth of winter.

My travels into those parts were the more irksome to me from the solitariness I underwent, and want of suitable society. For my business lying among the tenants, who were a rustic sort of people of various persuasions and humours, but not Friends, I had little opportunity of conversing with Friends, though I contrived to be with them as much as I could, especially on the first day of the week.

But that which made my present journey more heavy to me was a sorrowful exercise which was newly fallen upon me from my father.

He had, upon my first acquainting him with my inclination to marry, and to whom, not only very much approved the match, and voluntarily offered, without my either asking or expecting, to give me a handsome portion at present, with assurance of an addition to it hereafter. And he not only made this offer to me in private, but came down from London into the country on purpose, to be better acquainted with my friend, and did there make the same proposal to her; offering also to give security to any friend or relation of hers for the performance. Which offer she most generously declined, leaving him as free as she found him. But after we were married, notwithstanding such his promise, he wholly declined the performance of it, under pretence of our not being married by the priest and liturgy. This usage and evil treatment of us thereupon was a great trouble to me; and when I endeavoured to soften him in the matter, he forbade my speaking to him of it any more, and removed his lodging that I might not find him.

The grief I conceived on this occasion was not for any disappointment to myself or to my wife, for neither she nor I had any strict or necessary dependence upon that promise; but my grief was for the cause assigned by him as the ground of it, which was that our marriage was not by priest or liturgy.

And surely hard would it have been for my spirit to have borne up under the weight of this exercise, had not the Lord been exceeding gracious to me, and supported me with the inflowings of his love and life, wherewith he visited my soul in my travail. The sense whereof raised in my heart a thankful remembrance of his manifold kindnesses in his former dealings with me; and in the evening, when I came to my inn, while supper was getting ready, I took my pen and put into words what had in the day revolved in my thoughts. And thus it was

A SONG OF PRAISE.

Thy love, dear Father, and thy tender care,
  Have in my heart begot a strong desire
To celebrate Thy Name with praises rare,
  That others too Thy goodness may admire,
  And learn to yield to what Thou dost require.
Many have been the trials of my mind,
  My exercises great, great my distress;
Full oft my ruin hath my foe designed,
  My sorrows then my pen cannot express,
  Nor could the best of men afford redress.
When thus beset to Thee I lift mine eye,
  And with a mournful heart my moan did make;
How oft with eyes o'erflowing did I cry,
  "My God, my God, oh do me not forsake!
  Regard my tears! Some pity on me take!"
And to the glory of Thy holy name,
  Eternal God, whom I both love and fear,
I hereby do declare I never came
  Before Thy throne, and found Thee loth to hear,
  But always ready, with an open ear.
And though sometimes Thou seem'st Thy face to hide,
  As one that had withdrawn Thy love from me,
'Tis that my faith may to the full be tried,
  And that I thereby may the better see
  How weak I am when not upheld by Thee.
For underneath Thy holy arm I feel,
  Encompassing with strength as with a wall,
That, if the enemy trip up my heel,
  Thou ready art to save me from a fall:
  To Thee belong thanksgivings over all.
And for Thy tender love, my God, my King,
  My heart shall magnify Thee all my days,
My tongue of Thy renown shall daily sing,
  My pen shall also grateful trophies raise,
  As monuments to Thy eternal praise.

T. E.
KENT, *the Eleventh Month*, 1669.

Having finished my business in Kent, I struck off into Sussex, and finding the enemy endeavouring still more strongly to beset me, I betook myself to the Lord for safety, in whom I knew all help and strength was, and thus poured forth my supplication, directed

TO THE HOLY ONE.

Eternal God! preserver of all those
  (Without respect of person or degree)
Who in Thy faithfulness their trust repose,
  And place their confidence alone in Thee;
Be Thou my succour; for Thou know'st that I
On Thy protection, Lord, alone rely.
Surround me, Father, with Thy mighty power,
  Support me daily by Thine holy arm,
Preserve me faithful in the evil hour,
  Stretch forth Thine hand to save me from all harm.
Be Thou my helmet, breast–plate, sword, and shield,
And make my foes before Thy power yield.
Teach me the spiritual battle so to fight,
  That when the enemy shall me beset,
Armed cap–a–pie with the armour of Thy light,
  A perfect conquest o'er him I may get;
And with Thy battle–axe may cleave the head
Of him who bites that part whereon I tread.
Then being from domestic foes set free,
  The cruelties of men I shall not fear;
But in Thy quarrel, Lord, undaunted be,
  And for Thy sake the loss of all things bear;
Yea, though in dungeon locked, with joy will sing

An ode of praise to Thee, my God, my King.

T. E.
SUSSEX, *the Eleventh Month*, 1669.

As soon as I had dispatched the business I went about, I returned home without delay, and to my great comfort found my wife well, and myself very welcome to her; both which I esteemed as great favours.

Towards the latter part of the summer following I went into Kent again, and in my passage through London received the unwelcome news of the loss of a very hopeful youth who had formerly been under my care for education. It was Isaac Penington, the second son of my worthy friends Isaac and Mary Penington, a child of excellent natural parts, whose great abilities bespoke him likely to be a great man, had he lived to be a man. He was designed to be bred a merchant, and before he was thought ripe enough to be entered thereunto, his parents, at somebody's request, gave leave that he might go a voyage to Barbadoes, only to spend a little time, see the place, and be somewhat acquainted with the sea, under the care and conduct of a choice friend and sailor, John Grove, of London, who was master of a vessel, and traded to that island; and a little venture he had with him, made up by divers of his friends and by me among the rest. He made the voyage thither very well, found the watery element agreeable, had his health there, liked the place, was much pleased with his entertainment there, and was returning home with his little cargo, in return for the goods he carried out, when on a sudden, through unwariness, he dropped overboard, and, the vessel being under sail with a brisk gale, was irrecoverably lost, notwithstanding the utmost labour, care, and diligence of the master and sailors to have saved him.

This unhappy accident took from the afflicted master all the pleasure of his voyage, and he mourned for the loss of this youth as if it had been his own, yea only, son; for as he was in himself a man of a worthy mind, so the boy, by his witty and handsome behaviour in general, and obsequious carriage towards him in particular, had very much wrought himself into his favour.

As for me, I thought it one of the sharpest strokes I had met with, for I both loved the child very well and had conceived great hopes of general good from him; and it pierced me the deeper to think how deeply it would pierce his afflicted parents.

Sorrow for this disaster was my companion in this journey, and I travelled the roads under great exercise of mind, revolving in my thoughts the manifold accidents which the life of man was attended with and subject to, and the great uncertainty of all human things; I could find no centre, no firm basis, for the mind of man to fix upon but the divine power and will of the Almighty. This consideration wrought in my spirit a sort of contempt of what supposed happiness or pleasure this world, or the things that are in and of it, can of themselves yield, and raised my contemplation higher; which, as it ripened and came to some degree of digestion, I breathed forth in mournful accents thus:–

SOLITARY THOUGHTS ON THE UNCERTAINTY OF HUMAN THINGS.
OCCASIONED BY THE SUDDEN LOSS OF A HOPEFUL YOUTH.

Transibunt cito, quæ vos mansura putatis.

Those things soon will pass away
Which ye think will always stay.

What ground, alas! has any man
  To set his heart on things below,
Which, when they seem most like to stand,
  Fly like an arrow from a bow?
    Things subject to exterior sense
    Are to mutation most propense.
If stately houses we erect,
  And therein think to take delight,
On what a sudden are we checked,
  And all our hopes made groundless quite!
    One little spark in ashes lays
    What we were building half our days.
If on estate an eye we cast,

And pleasure there expect to find,
A secret providential blast
  Gives disappointment to our mind:
    Who now's on top ere long may feel
    The circling motion of the wheel.
If we our tender babes embrace,
  And comfort hope in them to have,
Alas! in what a little space
  Is hope, with them, laid in the grave!
    Whatever promiseth content
    Is in a moment from us rent.
This world cannot afford a thing
  Which, to a well–composed mind,
Can any lasting pleasure bring,
  But in its womb its grave will find.
    All things unto their centre tend;
    What had {230} beginning will have end.
But is there nothing then that's sure
  For man to fix his heart upon—
Nothing that always will endure,
  When all these transient things are gone?
    Sad state! where man, with grief oppressed
    Finds nought whereon his mind may rest.
O yes; there is a God above,
  Who unto men is also nigh,
On whose unalterable love
  We may with confidence rely,
    No disappointment can befall
    Us, having him that's All in All.
If unto Him we faithful be,
  It is impossible to miss
Of whatsoever He shall see
  Conducible unto our bliss.
    What can of pleasure him prevent
    Who hath the fountain of content?
In Him alone if we delight,

    And in His precepts pleasure take,
We shall be sure to do aright—
   'Tis not His nature to forsake.
    A proper object's He alone,
    For man to set his heart upon.

Domino mens nixa quieta est.

The mind which upon God is stayed
Shall with no trouble be dismayed.

T. E.
KENT, *the 4th of the Seventh Month*, 1650.

A copy of the foregoing lines, enclosed in a letter of condolence, I sent by the first post into Buckinghamshire, to my dear friends the afflicted parents; and upon my return home, going to visit them, we sat down, and solemnly mixed our sorrows and tears together.

About this time, as I remember, it was that some bickerings happening between some Baptists and some of the people called Quakers, in or about High Wycombe, in Buckinghamshire, occasioned by some reflecting words a Baptist preacher had publicly uttered in one of their meetings there, against the Quakers in general, and William Penn in particular, it came at length to this issue, that a meeting for a public dispute was appointed, to be holden at West Wycombe, between Jeremy Ives, who espoused his brother's cause, and William Penn.

To this meeting, it being so near me, I went, rather to countenance the cause than for any delight I took in such work; for indeed I have rarely found the advantage equivalent to the trouble and danger arising from those contests; for which cause I would not choose them, as, being justly engaged, I would not refuse them.

The issue of this proved better than I expected; for Ives, having undertaken an ill cause, to argue against the Divine light and universal grace conferred by God on all men, when he had spent his stock of arguments which he brought with him on that subject, finding

138

his work go on heavily and the auditory not well satisfied, stepped down from his seat and departed, with purpose to have broken up the assembly. But, except some few of his party who followed him, the people generally stayed, and were the more attentive to what was afterwards delivered amongst them; which Ives understanding, came in again, and in an angry, railing manner, expressing his dislike that we went not all away when he did, gave more disgust to the people.

After the meeting was ended, I sent to my friend Isaac Penington, by his son and servant, who returned home, though it was late, that evening, a short account of the business in the following distich:–

Prævaluit veritas: inimnici terga dedere;
Nos sumus in tuto; laus tribuenda Deo.

Which may be thus Englished:

Truth hath prevailed; the enemies did fly;
We are in safety; praise to God on high.

But both they and we had quickly other work found us: it soon became a stormy time. The clouds had been long gathering and threatening a tempest. The Parliament had sat some time before, and hatched that unaccountable law which was called the Conventicle Act; if that may be allowed to be called a law, by whomsoever made, which was so directly contrary to the fundamental laws of England, to common justice, equity, and right reason, as this manifestly was. For,

First, It broke down and overrun the bounds and banks anciently set for the defence and security of Englishmen's lives, liberties, and properties—viz., trial by juries; instead thereof, directing and authorizing justices of the peace, and that too privately out of sessions, to convict, fine, and by their warrants distrain upon offenders against it; directly contrary to the Great Charter.

Secondly, By that Act the informers, who swear for their own advantage, as being thereby entitled to a third part of the fines, were many times concealed, driving on an underhand private trade; so that men might be, and often were, convicted and fined, without having any notice or knowledge of it till the officers came and took away their goods, nor even then could they tell by whose evidence they were convicted; than which what could be more opposite to common justice, which requires that every man should be openly charged and have his accuser face to face, that he might both answer for himself before he be convicted, and object to the validity of the evidence given against him?

Thirdly, By that Act the innocent were punished for the offences of the guilty. If the wife or child was convicted of having been at one of those assemblies which by that Act was adjudged unlawful, the fine was levied on the goods of the husband or father of such wife or child, though he was neither present at such assembly, nor was of the same religious persuasion that they were of, but perhaps an enemy to it.

Fourthly, It was left in the arbitrary pleasure of the justices to lay half the fine for the house or ground where such assembly was holden, and half the fine for a pretended unknown preacher, and the whole fines of such and so many of the meeters as they should account poor, upon any other or others of the people who were present at the same meeting, not exceeding a certain limited sum; without any regard to equity or reason. And yet, such blindness doth the spirit of persecution bring on men, otherwise sharp−sighted enough, that this unlawful, unjust, unequal, unreasonable, and unrighteous law took place in almost all places, and was rigorously prosecuted against the meetings of Dissenters in general, though the brunt of the storm fell most sharply on the people called Quakers; not that it seemed to be more particularly levelled at them, but that they stood more fair, steady, and open, as a butt to receive all the shot that came, while some others found means and freedom to retire to coverts for shelter.

No sooner had the bishops obtained this law for suppressing all other meetings but their own, but some of the clergy of most ranks, and some others too who were overmuch bigoted to that party, bestirred themselves with might and main to find out and encourage the most profligate wretches to turn informers, and to get such persons into parochial offices as would be most obsequious to their commands, and ready at their beck to put it into the most rigorous execution. Yet it took not alike in all places, but some were forwarder in the work than others, according as the agents intended to be chiefly employed therein had been predisposed thereunto.

For in some parts of the nation care had been timely taken, by some not of the lowest rank, to choose out some particular persons—men of sharp wit, close countenances, pliant tempers, and deep dissimulation— and send them forth among the sectaries, so called, with instructions to thrust themselves into all societies, conform to all or any sort of religious profession, Proteus–like change their shapes, and transform themselves from one religious appearance to another as occasion should require. In a word, to be all things to all—not that they might win some, but that they might, if possible, ruin all; at least many.

The drift of this design was, that they who employed them might by this means get a full account what number of Dissenters' meetings, of every sort, there were in each county, and where kept; what number of persons frequented them, and of what rank; who amongst them were persons of estate, and where they lived; that when they should afterwards have troubled the waters, they might the better know where with most advantage to cast their nets.

He of these emissaries whose post was assigned him in this county of Bucks adventured to thrust himself upon a Friend under the counterfeit appearance or a Quaker, but being by the Friend suspected, and thereupon dismissed unentertained, he was forced to betake himself to an inn or alehouse for accommodation. Long he had not been there ere his unruly nature, not to be long kept under by the curb of a feigned society, broke forth into open profaneness; so true is that of the poet,

Naturam expellas furca licet, usque recurret.

To fuddling now falls he with those whom he found tippling there before, and who but he amongst them in him was then made good the proverb, *in vino veritas*, for in his cups he out with that which was no doubt to have been kept a secret. 'Twas to his pot companions that, after his head was somewhat heated with strong liquors, he discovered that he was sent forth by Dr. Mew, the then Vice–Chancellor of Oxford, on the design before related, and under the protection of Justice Morton, a warrant under whose hand and seal he there produced.

Sensible of his error too late, when sleep had restored him to some degree of sense, and discouraged with this ill success of his attempt upon the Quakers, he quickly left that place, and crossing through the country, cast himself among the Baptists at a meeting which they held in a private place, of which the over–easy credulity of some that went among them, whom he had craftily insinuated himself into, had given him notice. The entertainment he found amongst them deserved a better return than he made them; for, having smoothly wrought himself into their good opinion, and cunningly drawn some of them into an unwary openness and freedom of conversation with him upon the unpleasing subject of the severity of those times, he most villainously impeached one of them, whose name was —– Headach, a man well reputed amongst his neighbours, of having spoken treasonable words, and thereby brought the man in danger of losing both his estate and life, had not a seasonable discovery of his abominable practices elsewhere, imprinting terror, the effect of guilt, upon him, caused him to fly both out of the court and country at that very instant of time when the honest man stood at the bar ready to be arraigned upon his false accusation.

This his false charge against the Baptist left him no further room to play the hypocrite in those parts; off therefore go his cloak and vizor. And now he openly appears in his proper colours, to disturb the assemblies of God's people, which was indeed the very end for which the design at first was laid.

But because the law provided that a conviction must be grounded upon the oaths of two witnesses, it was needful for him, in order to the carrying on his intended mischief, to find out an associate who might be both sordid enough for such an employment and vicious enough to be his companion.

This was not an easy task, yet he found out one who had already given an experiment of his readiness to take other men's goods, being not long before released out of Aylesbury gaol, where he very narrowly escaped the gallows for having stolen a cow.

The names of these fellows being yet unknown in that part of the country where they began their work, the former, by the general voice of the country, was called the Trepan; the latter, the Informer, and from the colour of his hair Red–hair. But in a little time the Trepan called himself John Poulter, adding withal that Judge Morton used to call him John for the King, and that the Archbishop of Canterbury had given him a deaconry. That his name was indeed John Poulter, the reputed son of one —– Poulter, a butcher in

Salisbury, and that he had long since been there branded for a fellow egregiously wicked and debauched, we were assured by the testimony of a young man then living in Amersham, who both was his countryman and had known him in Salisbury, as well as by a letter from an inhabitant of that place, to whom his course of life had been well known.

His comrade, who for some time was only called the Informer, was named Ralph Lacy, of Risborough, and surnamed the Cow−stealer.

These agreed between themselves where to make their first onset, which was to be, and was, on the meeting of the people called Quakers, then holden at the house of William Russell, called Jourdan's, in the parish of Giles Chalfont, in the county of Bucks; that which was wanting to their accommodation was a place of harbour, for assistance wherein recourse was had to Parson Philips, none being so ready, none so willing, none so able to help them as he.

A friend he had in a corner, a widow woman, not long before one of his parishioners; her name was Anne Dell, and at that time she lived at a farm called Whites, a bye−place in the parish of Beaconsfield, whither she removed from Hitchindon. To her these fellows were recommended by her old friend the parson. She with all readiness received them; her house was at all times open to them; what she had was at their command.

Two sons she had at home with her, both at man's estate. The younger son, whose name was John Dell, listed himself in the service of his mother's new guests, to attend on them as their guide, and to inform them (who were too much strangers to pretend to know the names of any of the persons there) whom they should inform against.

Thus consorted, thus in a triple league confederated, on the 24th day of the fifth month, commonly called July, in the year 1670, they appeared openly, and began to act their intended tragedy upon the Quakers' meeting at the place aforesaid, to which I belonged, and at which I was present. Here the chief actor, Poulter, behaved himself with such impetuous violence and brutish rudeness as gave occasion for inquiry who or what he was? And being soon discovered to be the Trepan, so infamous and abhorred by all sober people, and afterwards daily detected of gross impieties and the felonious taking of certain goods from one of Brainford, whom also he cheated of money—these things raising an outcry in the country upon him, made him consult his own safety, and leaving his part to be acted by others, quitted the country as soon as he could.

He being gone, Satan soon supplied his place by sending one Richard Aris, a broken ironmonger of Wycombe, to join with Lacy in this service, prompted thereto in hopes that he might thereby repair his broken fortune.

Of this new adventurer this single character may serve, whereby the reader may make judgment of him as of the lion by his paw; that at the sessions held at Wycombe in October then last past he was openly accused of having enticed one Harding, of the same town, to be his companion and associate in robbing on the highway, and proof offered to be made that he had made bullets in order to that service; which charge Harding himself, whom he had endeavoured to draw into that heinous wickedness, was ready in court to prove upon oath had not the prosecution been discountenanced and smothered.

Lacy, the cow–stealer, having thus got Aris, the intended highwayman, to be his comrade, they came on the 21st of the month called August, 1670, to the meeting of the people called Quakers, where Lacy, with Poulter, had been a month before; and taking for granted that the same who had been there before were there then, they went to a justice of the peace called Sir Thomas Clayton, and swore at all adventure against one Thomas Zachary and his wife, whom Lacy understood to have been there the month before, that they were then present in that meeting; whereas neither the said Thomas Zachary nor his wife were at that meeting, but were both of them at London, above twenty miles distant, all that day, having been there some time before and after; which notwithstanding, upon this false oath of these false men, the Justice laid fines upon the said Thomas Zachary of £10 for his own offence, £10 for his wife's, and £10 for the offence of a pretended preacher, though indeed there was not any that preached at that meeting that day; and issued forth his warrant to the officers of Beaconsfield, where Thomas Zachary dwelt, for the levying of the same upon his goods.

I mention these things thus particularly, though not an immediate suffering of my own, because in the consequence thereof it occasioned no small trouble and exercise to me.

For when Thomas Zachary, returning home from London, understanding what had been done against him, and advising what to do, was informed by a neighbouring attorney that his remedy lay in appealing from the judgment of the convicting Justice to the general Quarter Sessions of the Peace, he thereupon ordering the said attorney to draw up his appeal in form of law, went himself with it, and tendered it to the Justice. But the Justice being a man neither well principled nor well natured, and uneasy that he should lose the advantage both of the present conviction and future service of such (in his judgment) useful men as those two bold informers were likely to be, fell sharply upon Thomas Zachary, charging him that he suffered justly, and that his suffering was not on a religious account.

This rough and unjust dealing engaged the good man to enter into further discourse with the Justice in defence of his own innocency; from which discourse the insidious Justice, taking offence at some expression of his, charged him with saying, "The righteous are oppressed, and the wicked go unpunished." Which the Justice interpreting to be a reflection on the Government, and calling it a high misdemeanour, required sureties of the good man to answer it at the next Quarter Sessions, and in the meantime to be bound to his good behaviour. But he, well knowing himself to be innocent of having broken any law, or done in this matter any evil, could not answer the Justice's unjust demand, and therefore was sent forthwith a prisoner to the county gaol.

By this severity it was thought the Justice designed not only to wreak his displeasure on this good man, but to prevent the further prosecution of his appeal; whereby he should at once both oppress the righteous by the levying of the fines unduly imposed upon him, and secure the informers from a conviction of wilful perjury and the punishment due therefor, that so they might go on without control in the wicked work they were engaged in.

But so great wickedness was not to be suffered to go unpunished, or at least undiscovered. Wherefore, although no way could be found at present to get the good man released from his unjust imprisonment, yet that his restraint might not hinder the prosecution of his appeal, on which the detection of the informer's villainy depended, consideration being had thereof amongst some Friends, the management of the prosecution was committed to my care, who was thought with respect at least to leisure and disengagement from other business, most fit to attend it; and very willingly I undertook it.

Wherefore at the next general Quarter Sessions of the Peace, held at High Wycombe in October following, I took care that four substantial witnesses, citizens of unquestionable credit, should come down from London in a coach and four horses, hired on purpose.

These gave so punctual and full evidence that Thomas Zachary and his wife were in London all that day whereon the informers had sworn them to have been at an unlawful meeting, at a place more than twenty miles distant from London, that notwithstanding what endeavours were used to the contrary, the jury found them not guilty. Whereupon the money deposited for the fines at the entering of the appeal ought to have been returned, and so were ten pounds of it; but the rest of the money being in the hand of the Clerk of the Peace, whose name was Wells, could never be got out again.

Thomas Zachary himself was brought from Aylesbury gaol to Wycombe, to receive his trial, and though no evil could be charged upon him, yet Justice Clayton, who at first committed him, displeased to see the appeal prosecuted and the conviction he had made set aside, by importunity prevailed with the bench to remand him to prison again, there to lie until another sessions.

While this was doing I got an indictment drawn up against the informers Aris and Lacy for wilful perjury, and caused it to be delivered to the grand jury, who found the bill. And although the court adjourned from the town—hall to the chamber at their inn, in favour as it was thought to the informers, on supposition we would not pursue them thither, yet thither they were pursued; and there being two counsel present from Windsor—(the name of the one was Starky, and of the other, as I remember, Forster, the former of whom I had before retained upon the trial of the appeal)—I now retained them both, and sent them into court again, to prosecute the informers upon this indictment; which they did so smartly that, the informers being present as not suspecting any such sudden danger, were of necessity called to the bar and arraigned, and having pleaded *Not Guilty*, were forced to enter a traverse to avoid a present commitment: all the favour the court could show them being to take them bail one for the other, though probably both not worth a groat, else they must have gone to gaol for want of bail, which would have put them besides their business, spoiled the informing trade, and broke the design; whereas now they were turned loose again to do what mischief they could until the next sessions.

Accordingly, they did what they could, and yet could make little or no earnings at it; for this little step of prosecution had made them so known, and their late apparent perjury had made them so detestable, that even the common sort of bad men shunned them, and would not willingly yield them any assistance.

146

The next Quarter Sessions was held at Aylesbury, whither we were fain to bring down our witnesses again from London, in like manner and at like charge, at the least, as before. And though I met with great discouragements in the prosecution, yet I followed it so vigorously that I got a verdict against the informers for wilful perjury, and had forthwith taken them up, had not they forthwith fled from justice and hid themselves. However, I moved by my attorney for an order of court, directed to all mayors, bailiffs, high constables, petty constables, and other inferior officers of the peace, to arrest and take them up wherever they should be found within the county of Bucks, and bring them to the county gaol.

The report of this so terrified them, that of all things dreading the misery of lying in a gaol, out of which they could not hope for deliverance otherwise than by at least the loss of their ears, they, hopeless now of carrying on their informing trade, disjoined, and one of them (Aris) fled the country; so that he appeared no more in this country. The other (Lacy) lurked privily for a while in woods and bye–places, until hunger and want forced him out; and then casting himself upon a hazardous adventure, which yet was the best, and proved to him best course he could have taken, he went directly to the gaol where he knew the innocent man suffered imprisonment by his means and for his sake; where asking for and being brought to Thomas Zachary, he cast himself on his knees at his feet, and with appearance of sorrow confessing his fault, did so earnestly beg for forgiveness that he wrought upon the tender nature of that very good man, not only to put him in hopes of mercy, but to be his advocate by letter to me, to mitigate at least, if not wholly to remit, the prosecution. To which I so far only consented as to let him know I would suspend the execution of the warrant upon him according as he behaved himself, or until he gave fresh provocation; at which message the fellow was so overjoyed that, relying with confidence thereon, he returned openly to his family and labour, and applied himself to business, as his neighbours observed and reported, with greater diligence and industry than he had ever done before.

Thus began and thus ended the informing trade in these parts of the county of Bucks; the ill success these first informers found discouraging all others, how vile soever, from attempting the like enterprise there ever after. And though it cost some money to carry on the prosecution, and some pains too, yet for every shilling so spent a pound probably might be saved of what in all likelihood would have been lost by the spoil and havoc that might have been made by distresses taken on their informations.

147

But so angry was the convicting Justice, whatever others of the same rank were, at this prosecution, and the loss thereby of the service of those honest men, the perjured informers—for, as I heard an attorney (one Hitchcock, of Aylesbury, who was their advocate in court) say, "A great lord, a peer of the realm, called them so in a letter directed to him; whereby he recommended to him the care and defence of them and their cause"—that he prevailed to have the oath of allegiance tendered in court to Thomas Zachary, which he knew he would not take because he could not take any oath at all; by which snare he was kept in prison a long time after, and, so far as I remember, until a general pardon released him.

But though it pleased the Divine Providence, which sometimes vouchsafeth to bring good out of evil, to put a stop, in a great measure at least, to the prosecution here begun, yet in other parts, both of the city and country, it was carried on with very great severity and rigour; the worst of men for the most part being set up for informers; the worst of magistrates encouraging and abetting them; and the worst of the priests who first began to blow the fire, now seeing how it took, spread, and blazed, clapping their hands, and hallooing them on to this evil work.

The sense whereof, as it deeply affected my heart with a sympathizing pity for the oppressed sufferers, so it raised in my spirit a holy disdain and contempt of that spirit and its agent by which this ungodly work was stirred up and carried on; which at length broke forth in an expostulatory poem, under the title of "Gigantomachia" (the Wars of the Giants against Heaven), not without some allusion to the second Psalm; thus:–

   Why do the heathen in a brutish rage,
Themselves against the Lord of Hosts engage?
Why do the frantic people entertain
Their thoughts upon a thing that is so vain?
Why do the kings themselves together set?
And why do all the princes them abet?
Why do the rulers to each other speak
After this foolish manner, "Let us break
Their bonds asunder; come, let us make haste,
With joint consent, their cords from us to cast?"

Why do they thus join hands, and counsel take
Against the Lord's Anointed? This will make
Him doubtless laugh who doth in heaven sit;
The Lord will have them in contempt for it.
His sore displeasure on them He will wreak,
And in His wrath will He unto them speak.
For on His holy hill of Sion He
His king hath set to reign: sceptres must be
Cast down before Him; diadems must lie
At foot of Him who sits in majesty
Upon His throne of glory; whence He will
Send forth His fiery ministers to kill
All those His enemies who would not be
Subject to His supreme authority.

   Where then will ye appear who are so far
From being subjects that ye rebels are
Against His holy government, and strive
Others from their allegiance too to drive?
What earthly prince such an affront would bear
From any of his subjects, should they dare
So to encroach on his prerogative?
Which of them would permit that man to live?
What should it be adjudged but treason? and
Death he must suffer for it out of hand.

   And shall the King of kings such treason see
Acted against Him, and the traitors be
Acquitted? No: vengeance is His, and they
That Him provoke shall know He will repay.

   And of a truth provoked He hath been
In a high manner by this daring sin
Of usurpation, and of tyranny
Over men's consciences, which should be free
To serve the living God as He requires,
And as His Holy Spirit them inspires.
For conscience is an inward thing, and none
Can govern that aright but God alone.

Nor can a well–informed conscience lower
Her sails to any temporary power,
Or bow to men's decrees; for that would be
Treason in a superlative degree;
For God alone can laws to conscience give,
And that's a badge of His prerogative.
  This is the controversy of this day
Between the holy God and sinful clay.
God hath throughout the earth proclaim'd that He
Will over conscience hold the sovereignty,
That He the kingdom to Himself will take,
And in man's heart His residence will make,
From whence His subjects shall such laws receive
As please His Royal Majesty to give.
  Man heeds not this, but most audaciously
Says, "Unto me belongs supremacy;
And all men's consciences within my land,
Ought to be subject unto my command."
  God by His Holy Spirit doth direct
His people how to worship; and expect
Obedience from them. Man says: "I ordain,
That none shall worship in that way, on pain
Of prison, confiscation, banishment,
Or being to the stake or gallows sent.
  God out of Babylon doth people call,
Commands them to forsake her ways, and all
Her several sorts of worship, to deny
Her whole religion as idolatry.
  Will man thus his usurped power forego,
And lose his ill–got government? Oh no:
But out comes his enacted, be it "That all
Who when the organs play will not downfall
Before this golden image, and adore
What I have caused to be set up therefor,
Into the fiery furnace shall be cast,
And be consumed with a flaming blast.

Or in the mildest terms conform, or pay
So much a month or so much every day,
Which we will levy on you by distress,
Sparing nor widow nor the fatherless;
And if you have not what will satisfy,
Ye're like in prison during life to lie."
Christ says, swear not; but man says, "Swear [or lie]
In prison, premunired, until you die."
Man's ways are, in a word, as opposite
To God's as midnight darkness is to light;
And yet fond man doth strive with might and main
By penal laws God's people to constrain
To worship what, when, where, how he thinks fit,
And to whatever he enjoins, submit.
    What will the issue of this contest be?
Which must give place—the Lord's or man's decree?
Will man be in the day of battle found
Able to keep the field, maintain his ground,
Against the mighty God? No more than can
The lightest chaff before the winnowing fan;
No more than straw could stand before the flame,
Or smallest atoms when a whirlwind came.
    The Lord, who in creation only said,
"Let us make man," and forthwith man was made,
Can in a moment by one blast of breath
Strike all mankind with an eternal death.
How soon can God all man's devices squash,
And with His iron rod in pieces dash
Him, like a potter's vessel? None can stand
Against the mighty power of His hand.
    Be therefore wise, ye kings, instructed be,
Ye rulers of the earth, and henceforth see
Ye serve the Lord in fear, and stand in awe
Of sinning any more against His law,
His royal law of liberty: to do
To others as you'd have them do to you.

Oh stoop, ye mighty monarchs, and let none
Reject His government, but kiss the Son
While's wrath is but a little kindled, lest
His anger burn, and you that have transgressed
His law so oft, and would not Him obey,
Eternally should perish from the way—
The way of God's salvation, where the just
Are blessed who in the Lord do put their trust.

Felix quem faciunt aliena pericula cautum.

    Happy's he
Whom others' harms do wary make to be.

As the unreasonable rage and furious violence of the persecutors had drawn the former expostulation from me, so in a while after, my heart being deeply affected with a sense of the great loving–kindness and tender goodness of the Lord to his people, in bearing up their spirits in their greatest exercises, and preserving them through the sharpest trials in a faithful testimony to his blessed truth, and opening in due time a door of deliverance to them, I could not forbear to celebrate His praises in the following lines, under the title of—

A SONG OF THE MERCIES AND DELIVERANCES OF THE LORD.

Had not the Lord been on our side,
  May Israel now say,
We were not able to abide
  The trials of that day
When men did up against us rise,
  With fury, rage, and spite,
Hoping to catch us by surprise,
  Or run us down by might.

Then had not God for us arose,
  And shown His mighty power,
We had been swallowed by our foes,
  Who waited to devour.
When the joint powers of death and hell
  Against us did combine,
And with united forces fell
  Upon us, with design
To root us out, then had not God
  Appeared to take our part,
And them chastized with His rod,
  And made them feel the smart,
We then had overwhelmed been
  And trodden in the mire;
Our enemies on us had seen
  Their cruel hearts' desire.
When stoned, when stocked, when rudely stripped,
  Some to the waist have been
(Without regard of sex), and whipped,
  Until the blood did spin;
Yea, when their skins with stripes looked black,
  Their flesh to jelly beat,
Enough to make their sinews crack,
  The lashes were so great;
Then had not God been with them to
  Support them, they had died,
His power it was that bore them through,
  Nothing could do't beside.
When into prisons we were thronged
  (Where pestilence was rife)
By bloody−minded men that longed
  To take away our life;
Then had not God been with us, we
  Had perished there no doubt
'Twas He preserved us there, and He
  It was that brought us out.

153

When sentenced to banishment
  Inhumanly we were,
To be from native country sent,
  From all that men call dear;
Then had not God been pleased t' appear,
  And take our cause in hand,
And struck them with a panic fear,
  Which put them to a stand:
Nay, had He not great judgments sent,
  And compassed them about,
They were at that time fully bent
  To root us wholly out.
Had He not gone with them that went,
  The seas had been their graves
Or when they came where they were sent,
  They had been sold for slaves.
But God was pleased still to give
  Them favour where they came,
And in His truth they yet do live
  To praise His Holy Name.
And now afresh do men contrive
  Another wicked way
Of our estates us to deprive,
  And take our goods away.
But will the Lord (who to this day
  Our part did always take)
Now leave us to be made a prey,
  And that too for His sake?
Can any one who calls to mind
  Deliverances past,
Discouraged be at what's behind,
  And murmur now at last?
Oh that no unbelieving heart
  Among us may be found,
That from the Lord would now depart,
  And coward–like give ground.

For without doubt the God we serve
  Will still our cause defend,
If we from Him do never swerve,
  But trust Him to the end.
What if our goods by violence
  From us be torn, and we
Of all things but our innocence
  Should wholly stripped be?
Would this be more than did befall
  Good Job? Nay sure, much less:
He lost estate, children and all,
  Yet he the Lord did bless.
But did not God his stock augment
  Double what 'twas before?
And this was writ to the intent
  That we should hope the more.
View but the lilies of the field,
  That neither knit nor spin,
Who is it that to them doth yield
  The robes they are decked in
Doth not the Lord the ravens feed,
  And for the sparrows care?
And will not He for His own seed
  All needful things prepare?
The lions shall sharp hunger bear,
  And pine for lack of food;
But who the Lord do truly fear,
  Shall nothing want that's good.
Oh! which of us can now diffide
  That God will us defend,
Who hath been always on our side,
  And will be to the end.

Spes confisa Deo nunquam confusa recedet.

155

Hope which on God is firmly grounded
Will never fail, nor be confounded.

Scarce was the before–mentioned storm of outward persecution from the Government blown over when Satan raised another storm of another kind against us on this occasion. The foregoing storm of persecution, as it lasted long, so in many parts of the nation, and particularly at London, it fell very sharp and violent especially on the Quakers. For they having no refuge but God alone to fly unto, could not dodge and shift to avoid the suffering as others of other denominations could, and in their worldly wisdom and policy did, altering their meetings with respect both to place and time, and forbearing to meet when forbidden or kept out of their meeting–houses. So that of the several sorts of Dissenters the Quakers only held up a public testimony as a standard or ensign of religion, by keeping their meetings duly and fully at the accustomed times and places so long as they were suffered to enjoy the use of their meeting–houses, and when they were shut up and Friends kept out of them by force, they assembled in the streets as near to their meeting–houses as they could.

This bold and truly Christian behaviour in the Quakers disturbed and not a little displeased the persecutors, who, fretting, complained that the stubborn Quakers broke their strength and bore off the blow from those other Dissenters whom, as they most feared, so they principally aimed at. For indeed the Quakers they rather despised than feared, as being a people from whose peaceable principles and practices they held themselves secure from danger; whereas having suffered severely, and that lately too, by and under the other Dissenters, they thought they had just cause to be apprehensive of danger from them, and good reason to suppress them.

On the other hand, the more ingenuous amongst other Dissenters of each denomination, sensible of the ease they enjoyed by our bold and steady suffering, which abated the heat of the persecutors and blunted the edge of the sword before it came to them, frankly acknowledged the benefit received; calling us the bulwark that kept off the force of the stroke from them, and praying that we might be preserved and enabled to break the strength of the enemy, nor could some of them forbear, those especially who were called Baptists, to express their kind and favourable opinion of us, and of the principles we professed, which emboldened us to go through that which but to hear of was a terror to

156

them.

This their good–will raised ill–will in some of their teachers against us, who though willing to reap the advantage of a shelter, by a retreat behind us during the time that the storm lasted, yet partly through an evil emulation, partly through fear lest they should lose some of those members of their society who had discovered such favourable thoughts of our principles and us, they set themselves as soon as the storm was over to represent us in as ugly a dress and in as frightful figure to the world as they could invent and put upon us.

In order whereunto, one Thomas Hicks, a preacher among the Baptists at London, took upon him to write several pamphlets successively under the title of "A Dialogue between a Christian and a Quaker," which were so craftily contrived that the unwary reader might conclude them to be not merely fictions, but real discourses actually held between one of the people called a Quaker and some other person. In these feigned dialogues, Hicks, having no regard to justice or common honesty, had made his counterfeit Quaker say whatsoever he thought would render him one while sufficiently erroneous, another while ridiculous enough, forging in the Quaker's name some things so abominably false, other things so intolerably foolish, as could not reasonably be supposed to have come into the conceit, much less to have dropped from the lip or pen of any that went under the name of a Quaker.

These dialogues, shall I call them, or rather diabologues, were answered by our friend William Penn in two books; the first being entitled "Reason against Railing," the other "The Counterfeit Christian Detected;" in which Hicks being charged with manifest as well as manifold forgeries, perversions, downright lies, and slanders against the people called Quakers in general, William Penn, George Whitehead, and divers others by name, complaint was made, by way of an appeal, to the Baptists in and about London for justice against Thomas Hicks.

Those Baptists, who it seems were in the plot with Hicks to defame at any rate, right or wrong, the people called Quakers, taking advantage of the absence of William Penn and George Whitehead, who were the persons most immediately concerned, and who were then gone a long journey on the service of truth, to be absent from the city, in all probability, for a considerable time, appointed a public meeting in one of their meeting–houses, under pretence of calling Thomas Hicks to account and hearing the

157

charge made good against him, but with design to give the greater stroke to the Quakers, when they, who should make good the charge against Hicks, could not be present. For upon their sending notice to the lodgings of William Penn and George Whitehead of their intended meeting, they were told by several Friends that both William Penn and George Whitehead were from home, travelling in the countries, uncertain where, and therefore could not be informed of their intended meeting, either by letter or express, within the time by them limited, for which reason they were desired to defer the meeting till they could have notice of it and time to return, that they might be at it. But these Baptists, whose design was otherwise laid, would not be prevailed with to defer their meeting, but, glad of the advantage, gave their brother Hicks opportunity to make a colourable defence where he had his party to help him and none to oppose him; and having made a mock show of examining him and his works of darkness, they, in fine, having heard one side, acquitted him.

This gave just occasion for a new complaint and demand of justice against him and them. For as soon as William Penn returned to London, he in print exhibited his complaint of this unfair dealing, and demanded justice by a rehearing of the matter in a public meeting to be appointed by joint agreement. This went hardly down with the Baptists, nor could it be obtained from them without great importunity and hard pressing. At length, after many delays and tricks used to shift it off, constrained by necessity, they yielded to have a meeting at their own meeting–house in Barbican, London.

There, amongst other Friends, was I, and undertook to read our charge there against Thomas Hicks, which not without much difficulty I did; they, inasmuch as the house was theirs, putting all the inconveniences they could upon us.

The particular passages and management of this meeting, as also of that other which followed soon after, they refusing to give us any other public meeting, we were fain to appoint in our own meeting–house, by Wheeler Street, near Spitalfields, London, and gave them timely notice of, I forbear here to mention; there being in print a narrative of each, to which for particular information I refer the reader.

But to this meeting Thomas Hicks would not come, but lodged himself at an alehouse hard by; yet sent his brother Ives, with some others of the party, by clamorous noises to divert us from the prosecution of our charge against him; which they so effectually performed that they would not suffer the charge to be heard, though often attempted to be read.

As this rude behaviour of theirs was a cause of grief to me, so afterwards, when I understood that they used all evasive tricks to avoid another meeting with us, and refused to do us right, my spirit was greatly stirred at their injustice, and in the sense thereof, willing, if possible, to have provoked them to more fair and manly dealing. I let fly a broadside at them, in a single sheet of paper, under the title of "A Fresh Pursuit"; in which, having restated the controversy between them and us, and reinforced our charge of forgery, &c., against Thomas Hicks and his abettors, I offered a fair challenge to them, not only to Thomas Hicks himself, but to all those his compurgators who had before undertaken to acquit him from our charge, together with their companion Jeremy Ives, to give me a fair and public meeting, in which I would make good our charge against him as principal, and all the rest of them as accessories. But nothing could provoke them to come fairly forth.

Yet not long after, finding themselves galled by the narrative lately published of what had passed in the last meeting near Wheeler Street, they, to help themselves if they could, sent forth a counter–account of that meeting and of the former at Barbican, as much to the advantage of their own cause as they upon deliberate consideration could contrive it. This was published by Thomas Plant, a Baptist teacher, and one of Thomas Hicks' former compurgators, and bore (but falsely) the title of "A Contest for Christianity; or, a Faithful Relation of two late Meetings," &c.

To this I quickly wrote and published an answer; and because I saw the design and whole drift of the Baptists was to shroud Thomas Hicks from our charge of forgery under the specious pretence of his and their standing up and contending for Christianity, I gave my book this general title: "Forgery no Christianity; or, a Brief Examen of a late Book," &c. And having from their own book plainly convicted that which they called a "faithful relation" to be indeed a false relation, I, in an expostulatory postscript to the Baptists, reinforced our charge and my former challenge, offering to make it good against them before a public and free auditory. But they were too wary to appear further, either in person or in print.

This was the end of that controversy, which was observed to have this issue: that what those dialogues were written to prevent was by the dialogues, and their unfair, unmanly, unchristian carriage, in endeavouring to defend them, hastened and brought to pass; for not a few of the Baptists' members upon this occasion left their meetings and society, and came over to the Quakers' meetings and were joined in fellowship with them; thanks be to God.

The controversy which had been raised by those cavilling Baptists had not been long ended before another was raised by an Episcopal priest in Lincolnshire, who fearing, as it seemed, to lose some of his hearers to the Quakers, wrote a book which he miscalled, "A Friendly Conference between a Minister and a Parishioner of his inclining to Quakerism," in which he misstated and greatly perverted the Quakers' principles, that he might thereby beget in his parishioners an aversion to them; and that he might abuse us the more securely, he concealed himself, sending forth his book without a name.

This book coming to my hand, became my concern (after I had read it, and considered the evil management and worse design thereof) to answer it; which I did in a treatise called "Truth Prevailing, and Detecting Error," published in the year 1676.

My answer I divided, according to the several subjects handled in the conference, into divers distinct chapters, the last of which treated of Tithes.

This being the priests' Delilah, and that chapter of mine pinching them, it seems, in a tender part, the belly, they laid their heads together, and with what speed they could sent forth a distinct reply to the last chapter, "Of Tithes," in mine, under the title of "The Right of Tithes Asserted and Proved." This also came forth without a name, yet pretended to be written by another hand.

Before I had finished my rejoinder to this came forth another called "A Vindication of the Friendly Conference," said to be written by the author of the "Feigned Conference," who was not yet willing to trust the world with his name. So much of it as related to the subject I was then upon (Tithes) I took into my rejoinder to the "Right of Tithes," which I published in the year 1678, with this title: "The Foundation of Tithes Shaken," &c.

After this it was a pretty while before I heard from either of them again. But at length came forth a reply to my last, supposed to be written by the same hand who had before written "The Right of Tithes Asserted," &c., but still without a name. This latter book had more of art than argument in it. It was indeed a hash of ill–cooked cram set off with as much flourish as the author was master of, and swelled into bulk by many quotations;

but those so wretchedly misgiven, misapplied, or perverted, that to a judicious and impartial reader I durst oppose my "Foundation of Tithes Shaken" to the utmost force that book has in it. Yet it coming forth at a time when I was pretty well at leisure, I intended a full refutation thereof, and in order thereunto had written between forty and fifty sheets, when other business, more urgent, intervening, took me off, and detained me from it so long that it was then judged out of season, and so it was laid aside.

Hitherto the war I had been engaged in was in a sort foreign, with people of other religious persuasions, such as were open and avowed enemies; but now another sort of war arose, an intestine war, raised by some among ourselves—such as had once been of us, and yet retained the same profession, and would have been thought to be of us still; but having through ill–grounded jealousies let in discontents, and thereupon fallen into jangling, chiefly about church discipline, they at length broke forth into an open schism, headed by two Northern men of name and note, John Wilkinson and John Story; the latter of whom, as being the most active and popular man, having gained a considerable interest in the West, carried the controversy with him thither, and there spreading it, drew many, too many, to abet him therein.

Among those, William Rogers, a merchant of Bristol, was not the least, nor least accounted of by himself and some others. He was a bold and active man, moderately learned, but immoderately conceited of his own parts and abilities, which made him forward to engage, as thinking none would dare to take up the gauntlet he should cast down. This high opinion of himself made him rather a troublesome than formidable enemy.

That I may here step over the various steps by which he advanced to open hostility, as what I was not actually or personally engaged in: He in a while arrived to that height of folly and wickedness that he wrote and published a large book, in five parts, to which he maliciously gave for a title, "The Christian Quaker distinguished from the Apostate and Innovator," thereby arrogating to himself and those who were of his party the topping style of Christian Quaker, and no less impiously than uncharitably branding and rejecting all others, even the main body of Friends, for apostates and innovators.

When this book came abroad it was not a little (and he, for its sake) cried up by his injudicious admirers, whose applause setting his head afloat, he came up to London at the time of the yearly meeting then following, and at the close thereof gave notice in writing to this effect—viz., "That if any were dissatisfied with his book he was there ready to maintain and defend both it and himself against all comers."

This daring challenge was neither dreaded nor slighted, but an answer forthwith returned in writing, signed by a few Friends, amongst whom I was one, to let him know that, as many were dissatisfied with his book and him, he should not fail, God willing, to be met by the sixth hour next morning at the meeting–place at Devonshire House.

Accordingly we met, and continued the meeting till noon or after, in which time he, surrounded with those of his own party as might abet and assist him, was so fairly foiled and baffled, and so fully exposed, that he was glad to quit the place, and early next morning the town also, leaving, in excuse for his going so abruptly off, and thereby refusing us another meeting with him, which we had earnestly provoked him to, this slight shift, "That he had before given earnest for his passage in the stage–coach home, and was not willing to lose it."

I had before this gotten a sight of his book, and procured one for my use on this occasion, but I had not time to read it through; but a while after, Providence cast another of them into my hands very unexpectedly, for our dear friend George Fox passing through this country among Friends, and lying in his journey at my house, had one of them in his bag, which he had made some marginal notes upon. For that good man, like Julius Cæsar, willing to improve all parts of his time, did usually, even in his travels, dictate to his amanuensis what he would have committed to writing. I knew not that he had this book with him, for he had not said anything to me of it, till going in the morning into his chamber while he was dressing himself, I found it lying on the table by him; and understanding that he was going but for a few weeks to visit Friends in the meetings hereabouts and the neighbouring parts of Oxford and Berkshire, and so return through this county again, I made bold to ask him if he would favour me so much as to leave it with me till his return, that I might have the opportunity of reading it through. He consented, and as soon almost as he was gone I set myself to read it over. But I had not gone far in it ere, observing the many foul falsehoods, malicious slanders, gross perversions, and false doctrines abounding in it, the sense thereof inflamed my breast with a just and holy indignation against the work, and that devilish spirit in which it was brought forth; wherefore, finding my spirit raised and my understanding divinely opened to refute it, I began the book again, and reading it with pen in hand, answered it paragraphically as I went. And so clear were the openings I received from the Lord therein, that by the time my friend came back I had gone through the greatest part of it, and was too far engaged in spirit to think of giving over the work; wherefore, requesting him to continue the book a little longer with me, I soon after finished the answer, which, with Friends' approbation, was printed under the title of "An Antidote against the Infection of William Rogers' Book, miscalled 'The Christian Quaker, &c.'" This was written in the year 1682. But no answer was given to it, either by him or any other of his party, though many others were concerned therein, and some by name, so far as I have ever heard. Perhaps there might be the hand of Providence overruling them therein, to give me leisure to attend some other services which soon after fell upon me.

For it being a stormy time, and persecution waxing hot, upon the Conventicle Act, through the busy boldness of hungry informers, who for their own advantage did not only themselves hunt after religious and peaceable meetings, but drove on the officers, not only the more inferior and subordinate, but in some places even the justices also, for fear of penalties, to hunt with them and for them; I found a pressure upon my spirit to write a small treatise to inform such officers how they might secure and defend themselves from being ridden by those malapert informers, and made their drudges.

This treatise I called "A Caution to Constables and other inferior Officers concerned in the Execution of the Conventicle Act: with some Observations thereupon, humbly offered by way of Advice to such well-meaning and moderate Justices of the Peace as would not willingly ruin their peaceable Neighbours," &c.

This was thought to have some good service where it came upon such sober and moderate officers, as well justices as constables, &c., as acted rather by constraint than choice, by encouraging them to stand their ground with more courage and resolution against the insults of saucy informers.

But whatever ease it brought to others, it brought me some trouble, and had like to have brought me into more danger, had not Providence wrought my deliverance by an unexpected way.

For as soon as it came forth in print, which was in the year 1683, one William Ayrs, of Watford in Hertfordshire, a Friend, and an acquaintance of mine, who was both an apothecary and barber, being acquainted with divers of the gentry in those parts, and going often to some of their houses to trim them, took one of these books with him when he went to trim Sir Benjamin Titchborn of Rickmansworth, and presented it to him, supposing he would have taken it kindly, as in like cases he had formerly done. But it fell out otherwise. For he, looking it over after Ayrs was gone, and taking it by the wrong handle, entertained an evil opinion of it, and of me for it, though he knew me not.

He thereupon communicated both the book and his thoughts upon it to a neighbouring justice, living in Rickmansworth, whose name was Thomas Fotherly, who concurring with him in judgment, they concluded that I should be taken up and prosecuted for it as a seditious book; for a libel they could not call it, my name being to it at length.

Wherefore, sending for Ayrs, who had brought the book, Justice Titchborn examined him if he knew me, and where I dwelt; who telling him he knew me well, and had been often at my house, he gave him in charge to give me notice that I should appear before him and the other justice at Rickmansworth on such a day; threatening that if I did not appear, he himself should be prosecuted for spreading the book.

This put William Ayrs in a fright. Over he came in haste with his message to me, troubled that he should be a means to bring me into trouble; but I endeavoured to give him ease by assuring him I would not fail, with God's leave, to appear at the time and place appointed, and thereby free him from trouble or danger.

In the interim I received advice, by an express out of Sussex, that Guli Penn, with whom I had had an intimate acquaintance and firm friendship from our very youths, was very dangerously ill, her husband being then absent in Pennsylvania, and that she had a great desire to see and speak with me.

This put me to a great strait, and brought a sore exercise on my mind. I was divided betwixt honour and friendship. I had engaged my word to appear before the justices, which to omit would bring dishonour on me and my profession. To stay till that time was come and past might probably prove, if I should then be left at liberty, too late to answer her desire and satisfy friendship.

After some little deliberation, I resolved, as the best expedient to answer both ends, to go over next morning to the justices, and lay my strait before them, and try if I could procure from them a respite of my appearance before them until I had been in Essex, and paid the duty of friendship to my sick friend; which I had the more hopes to obtain, because I knew those justices had a great respect for Guli; for when William Penn and she were first married they lived for some years at Rickmansworth, in which time they contracted a neighbourly friendship with both these justices and theirs, who ever after retained a kind regard for them both.

Early therefore in the morning I rode over; but being wholly a stranger to the justices, I went first to Watford, that I might take Ayrs along with me, who supposed himself to have some interest in Justice Titchborn, and when I came there, understanding that another Friend of that town, whose name was John Wells, was well acquainted with the other Justice Fotherly, having imparted to them the occasion of my coming, I took them both with me, and hasted back to Rickmansworth, where having put our horses up at an inn, and leaving William Ayrs, who was a stranger to Fotherly, there, I went with John Wells to Fotherly's house, and being brought into a fair hall, I tarried there while Wells went into the parlour to him, and having acquainted him that I was there and desired to speak with him, brought him to me with severity in his countenance.

After he had asked me, in a tone which spoke displeasure, what I had to say to him, I told him I came to wait on him upon an intimation given me that he had something to say to me. He thereupon plucking my book out of his pocket, asked me if I owned myself to be the author of that book? I told him, if he pleased to let me look into it, if it were mine, I would not deny it. He thereupon giving it into my hand, when I had turned over the leaves and looked it through, finding it to be as it came from the press, told him I wrote the book, and would own it, all but the errors of the press. Whereupon he, looking sternly on me, answered, "Your own errors, you should have said."

Having innocency on my side, I was not at all daunted at either his speech or looks, but feeling the Lord present with me, I replied, "I know there are errors of the press in it, and therefore I excepted them; but I do not know there are any errors of mine in it, and therefore cannot except them. But," added I, "if thou pleasest to show me any error of mine in it, I shall readily both acknowledge and retract it;" and thereupon I desired him to give me an instance, in any one passage in that book, wherein he thought I had erred. He said he needed not go to particulars, but charge me with the general contents of the whole book. I replied that such a charge would be too general for me to give a particular answer to; but if he would assign me any particular passage or sentence in the book wherein he apprehended the ground of offence to lie, when I should have opened the terms, and explained my meaning therein, he might perhaps find cause to change his mind and entertain a better opinion both of the book and me. And therefore I again entreated him to let me know what particular passage or passages had given him an offence. He told me I needed not to be in so much haste for that—I might have it timely enough, if not too soon; "but this," said he, "is not the day appointed for your hearing, and therefore," added he, "what, I pray, made you in such haste to come now?" I told him I hoped he would not take it for an argument of guilt that I came before I was sent for, and offered myself to my purgation before the time appointed. And this I spake with somewhat a brisker air, which had so much influence on him as to bring a somewhat softer air over his countenance.

Then going on, I told him I had a particular occasion which induced me to come now, which was, that I received advice last night by an express out of Sussex, that William Penn's wife, with whom I had had an intimate acquaintance and strict friendship, *ab ipsis fere incunabilis*, {276a} at least *a teneris unguiculis*, {276b} lay now there very ill, not without great danger, in the apprehension of those about her, of her life, and that she had expressed her desire that I would come to her as soon as I could, the rather for that her husband was absent in America. That this had brought a great strait upon me, being divided between friendship and duty, willing to visit my friend in her illness, which the nature and law of friendship required, yet unwilling to omit my duty by failing of my appearance before him and the other justice, according to their command and my promise, lest I should thereby subject, not my own reputation only, but the reputation of my religious profession, to the suspicion of guilt, and censure of willingly shunning a trial. To prevent which I had chosen to anticipate the time, and came now to see if I could give them satisfaction in what they had to object against me, and thereupon being dismissed, pursue my journey into Sussex, or if by them detained, to submit to Providence, and by an express to acquaint my friend therewith, both to free her from an expectation of my coming and myself from any imputation of neglect.

While I thus delivered myself I observed a sensible alteration in the justice, and when I had done speaking, he first said he was very sorry for Madam Penn's illness, of whose virtue and worth he spoke very highly, yet not more than was her due; then he told me that for her sake he would do what he could to further my visit to her; "but," said he, "I am but one, and of myself can do nothing in it; therefore you must go to Sir Benjamin Titchborn, and if he be at home, see if you can prevail with him to meet me, that we may consider of it. But I can assure you," added he, "the matter which will be laid to your charge concerning your book is of greater importance than you seem to think it. For your book has been laid before the King and Council, and the Earl of Bridgewater, who is one of the Council, hath thereupon given us command to examine you about it, and secure you."

"I wish," said I, "I could speak with the Earl myself, for I make no doubt but to acquit myself unto him; and," added I, "if thou pleasest to give me thy letter to him, I will wait upon him with it forthwith. For although I know," continued I, "that he hath no favour for any of my persuasion, yet knowing myself to be wholly innocent in this matter, I can with confidence appear before him, or even before the King in Council."

"Well," said he, "I see you are confident; but for all that, let me tell you, how good soever your intention was, you timed the publishing of your book very unluckily, for you cannot be ignorant that there is a very dangerous plot lately discovered, contrived by the Dissenters against the Government and his Majesty's life." [This was the Rye plot, then newly broke forth, and laid upon the Presbyterians.] "And for you," added he, "to publish a book just at that juncture of time, to discourage the magistrates and other officers from putting in execution those laws which were made to suppress their meetings, looks, I must tell you, but with a scurvy countenance upon you."

"If," replied I, with somewhat a pleasanter air, "there was any mistiming in the case, it must lie on the part of those plotters for timing the breaking forth of their plot while my book was printing, for I can bring very good proof that my book was in the press and well–nigh wrought off before any man talked or knew of a plot, but those who were in it."

Here our discourse ended, and I, taking for the present my leave of him, went to my horse, and changing my companion, rode to Justice Titchborn's, having with me William Ayrs, who was best acquainted with him, and who had casually brought this trouble on me.

When he had introduced me to Titchborn, I gave him a like account of the occasion of my coming at that time as I had before given to the other Justice. And both he and his lady, who was present, expressed much concern for Guli Penn's illness.

I found this man to be of quite another temper than Justice Fotherly; for he was smooth, soft, and oily, whereas the other was rather rough, severe, and sharp. Yet at the winding–up I found Fotherly my truest friend.

When I had told Sir Benjamin Titchborn that I came from Justice Fotherly, and requested him to give him a meeting to consider of my business, he readily, without any hesitation, told me he would go with me to Rickmansworth, from which his house was distant about a mile, and calling for his horses, mounted immediately, and to Rickmansworth we rode.

After they had been a little while together, I was called in before them, and in the first place they examined me, "What was my intention and design in writing that book?" I told them the introductory part of it gave a plain account of it—viz., "That it was to get ease from the penalties of a severe law often executed with too great a severity by unskilful officers, who were driven on beyond the bounds of their duty by the impetuous threats of a sort of insolent fellows, as needy as greedy, who for their own advantage sought our ruin." To prevent which was the design and drift of that book, by acquainting such officers how they might safely demean themselves in the execution of their offices towards their honest and peaceable neighbours, without ruining either their neighbours or themselves to enrich some of the worst of men; and that I humbly conceived it was neither unlawful nor unreasonable for a sufferer to do this, so long as it was done in a fair, sober, and peaceable way.

They then put me in mind of the plot; told me it was a troublesome and dangerous time, and my book might be construed to import sedition, in discouraging the officers from putting the laws in execution, as by law and by their oath they were bound; and in fine brought it to this issue, that they were directed to secure me by a commitment to prison until the assize, at which I should receive a further charge than they were provided now to give me; but because they were desirous to forward my visit to Madam Penn, they told me they would admit me to bail, and therefore, if I would enter a recognisance, with sufficient sureties, for my appearance at the next assize, they would leave me at liberty to go on my journey.

I told them I could not do it. They said they would give me as little trouble as they could, and therefore they would not put me to seek bail, but would accept those two friends of mine who were then present, to be bound with me for my appearance.

I let them know my strait lay not in the difficulty of procuring sureties, for I did suppose myself to have sufficient acquaintance and credit in that place, if on such an occasion I could be free to use it; but as I knew myself to be an innocent man, I had not satisfaction in myself to desire others to be bound for me, nor to enter myself into a recognisance, that carrying in it, to my apprehension, a reflection on my innocency and the reputation of my Christian profession.

Here we stuck and struggled about this a pretty while, till at length finding me fixed in my judgment, and resolved rather to go to prison than give bail, they asked me if I was against appearing, or only against being bound with sureties to appear. I told them I was not against appearing, which as I could not avoid if I would, so I would not if I might; but was ready and willing to appear, if required, to answer whatsoever should be charged against me. But in any case of a religious nature, or wherein my Christian profession was concerned, which I took this case to be, I could not yield to give any other or further security than my word or promise as a Christian.

They, unwilling to commit me, took hold of that, and asked if I would promise to appear. I answered, "Yes; with due limitations."—"What do you mean by due limitations?" said they.—"I mean," replied I, "if I am not disabled or prevented by sickness or imprisonment. For," added I, "as you allege that it is a troublesome time, I perhaps may find it so. I may, for aught I know, be seized and imprisoned elsewhere on the same account for which I now stand here before you, and if I should, how then could I appear at the assize in this county?"—"Oh," said they, "these are due limitations indeed. Sickness or imprisonment are lawful excuses, and if either of these befall you, we shall not expect your appearance here; but then you must certify us that you are so disabled by sickness or restraint."

"But," said I, "how shall I know when and where I shall wait upon you again after my return from Sussex?"—"You need not," said they, "trouble yourself about that; we will take care to give you notice of both time and place, and till you hear from us you may dispose yourself as you please."

"Well, then," said I, "I do promise you that when I shall have received from you a fresh command to appear before you, I will, if the Lord permit me life, health, and liberty, appear when and where you shall appoint."

"It is enough," said they; "we will take your word." And desiring me to give their hearty respects and service to Madam Penn, they dismissed me with their good wishes for a good journey.

I was sensible that in this they had dealt very favourably and kindly with me, therefore I could not but acknowledge to them the sense I had thereof; which done, I took leave of them, and mounting, returned home with what haste I could, to let my wife know how I had sped. And having given her a summary account of the business, I took horse again, and went so far that evening towards Worminghurst that I got thither pretty early next morning, and to my great satisfaction found my friend in a hopeful way towards recovery.

I stayed some days with her, and then, finding her illness wear daily off, and some other Friends being come from London to visit her, I, mindful of my engagement to the Justices, and unwilling by too long an absence to give them occasion to suspect I was willing to avoid their summons, leaving those other Friends to bear her company longer, took my leave of her and them, and set my face homewards, carrying with me the welcome account of my friend's recovery.

Being returned home, I waited in daily expectation of a command from the Justices to appear again before them; but none came. I spoke with those Friends who had been with me when I was before them, and they said they had heard nothing of it from them, although they had since been in company with them. At length the assize came, but no notice was given to me that I should appear there: in fine, they never troubled themselves nor me any further about it.

Thus was a cloud, that looked black and threatened a great storm, blown gently over by a providential breath, which I could not but with a thankful mind acknowledge to the All–great, All–good, All–wise Disposer, in whose hand and at whose command the hearts of all men, even the greatest, are, and who turns their counsels, disappoints their purposes, and defeats their designs and contrivances as He pleases. For if my dear friend Guli Penn had not fallen sick, if I had not thereupon been sent for to her, I had not prevented the time of my appearance, but had appeared on the day appointed; and, as I afterwards understood, that was the day appointed for the appearance of a great many persons of the Dissenting party in that side of the country, who were to be taken up and secured on account of the aforementioned plot, which had been cast upon the Presbyterians. So that if I had then appeared with and amongst them, I had in all likelihood been sent to gaol with them for company, and that under the imputation of a plotter, than which nothing was more contrary to my profession and inclination.

But though I came off so easily, it fared not so well with others; for the storm increasing, many Friends in divers parts, both of city and country, suffered greatly; the sense whereof did deeply affect me, and the more for that I observed the magistrates, not thinking the laws which had been made against us severe enough, perverted the law in order to punish us. For calling our peaceable meetings riots, which in the legal notion of the word riot is a contradiction in terms, they indicted our friends as rioters for only sitting in a meeting, though nothing was there either said or done by them, and then set fines on them at pleasure.

This I knew to be not only against right and justice, but even against law; and it troubled me to think that we should be made to suffer not only by laws made directly against us, but even by laws that did not at all concern us. Nor was it long before I had occasion offered more thoroughly to consider this matter.

For a justice of the peace in this county, who was called Sir Dennis Hampson, of Taplow, breaking in with a party of horse upon a little meeting near Wooburn, in his neighbourhood, the 1st of the fifth month, 1683, sent most of the men, to the number of twenty−three, whom he found there, to Aylesbury prison, though most of them were poor men who lived by their labour; and not going himself to the next Quarter Sessions at Buckingham, on the 12th of the same month, sent his clerk with direction that they should be indicted for a riot. Whither the prisoners were carried and indicted accordingly, and being pressed by the court to traverse and give bail, they moved to be tried forthwith, but that was denied them. And they, giving in writing the reason of their refusing bail and fees, were remanded to prison till next Quarter Sessions; but William Woodhouse was again hailed, as he had been before, and William Mason and John Reeve, who not being Friends, but casually taken at that meeting, entered recognisance as the court desired, and so were released till next sessions; before which time Mason died, and Reeve being sick, appeared not, but got himself taken off. And in the eighth month following the twenty−one prisoners that remained were brought to trial; a jury was found, who brought in a pretended verdict that they were *guilty of a riot* for only sitting peaceably together without word or action, and though there was no proclamation made nor they required to depart. But one of the jurymen afterwards did confess he knew not what a riot was; yet the prisoners were fined a noble apiece, and recommitted to prison during life (a hard sentence) or the King's pleasure, or until they should pay the said fines. William Woodhouse was forthwith discharged by his kinsman's paying the fine and fees for him; Thomas Dell and Edward Moore also, by other people of the world paying their fines and fees; and shortly after, Stephen Pewsey, by the town and parish where he lived, for fear his wife and children should become a charge upon them. The other seventeen remained prisoners till King James's proclamation of pardon; whose names were Thomas and William Sexton, Timothy Child, Robert Moor, Richard James, William and Robert Aldridge, John Ellis, George Salter, John Smith, William Tanner, William Batchelor, John Dolbin, Andrew Brothers, Richard Baldwin, John Jennings, and Robert Austin.

Footnotes:

{180} Ille dolet vere, qui fine teste dolet.

{190} Rom. viii. 9

{230} Understand this of natural things.

{276a} Almost from our cradle.

{276b} From our tender age.

CPSIA information can be obtained at www.ICGtesting.com
Printed in the USA
LVOW111221151212

311777LV00004B/741/A